MOVING
to the
COUNTRY

GW00670573

MOVING
to the
COUNTRY

DAVID GREEN

KOGAN
PAGE

Copyright © David Green 1990

All rights reserved. No reproduction, copy or transmission of this
publication may be made without written permission.

No paragraph of this publication may be reproduced, copied or
transmitted save with written permission or in accordance with the
provisions of the Copyright Act 1956 (as amended), or under the
terms of any licence permitting limited copying issued by the
Copyright Licensing Agency, 7 Ridgmount Street,
London WC1E 7AE.

Any person who does any unauthorised act in relation to this
publication may be liable to criminal prosecution and civil claims for
damages.

First published in Great Britain in 1990 by
Kogan Page Limited, 120 Pentonville Road,
London N1 9JN.

British Library Cataloguing in Publication Data
Green, David, *1935–*
    Moving to the country.
    1. Great Britain. Rural regions. Social life
    I. Title
    941'.009'734

    ISBN 0-7494-0026-9 pbk

Typeset by DP Photosetting, Aylesbury, Bucks
Printed and bound in Great Britain by
Richard Clay, The Chaucer Press, Bungay

Contents

Preface

If you want to move to the country, are moving, or have moved, you will find this book useful and profitable. I hope you will also find it interesting, even if you are merely fond of country life.

Books like this are usually framed in personal experience and this one is no exception. I was nine when my family moved from my birthplace in the Isle of Wight to Manchester; twenty-three when I moved out of Manchester to Goostrey in mid-Cheshire; and thirty-eight when we moved to our present home – an isolated old farmhouse near the coast in West Wales.

It helps to have enough money if you want to move into the country but it is not always critical. My cottage in Goostrey had been condemned and my farmhouse in West Wales was semi-derelict by the time I bought them. I could not have afforded either had that not been so, or for that matter their restoration without doing most of it myself. And if chance had not taken me to these places shortly before prices rocketed with substantial inward migrations from urban areas, I could not have afforded them anyway.

Nor was I able to live in them without a lot of understanding from colleagues and a long apprenticeship in the art of commuting. Goostrey is 25 miles from the centre of Manchester and I travelled there and back for work each day for 11 years. West Wales is far more remote. Though my distant work was mostly part time, I continued working for a high technology industry in Warrington 186 miles away for seven years after our move there – a trip a week for 12 months; alternate weeks for another 12 months; and once a month after that. That certainly concentrated my mind on developing local and other options, and buying a computer in 1982 added significantly to them.

The large migrations which soon followed me into both places had different causes. In Goostrey it was the electrification of the main Manchester–Euston railway line (goodbye for ever to only two steam trains in and out on Sundays), the construction of the M6 motorway, and the expansion of Manchester Airport which opened up the village to people more rational than me – and doubled it out of rural somnolence in the space of six years. In West Wales it was the urban property price explosion between 1971 and 1973 which left many who had long hoped for a country life with the resources at last to achieve it. The comparable inflation between 1986 and 1988 has generated a new wave.

I count myself fortunate that the way things happened – twice – meant that I ended up with some splendid friends both among those long native to the places into which I moved, and among those who afterwards flowed into them. Never was I more grateful for that friendship than when, out of the blue, my wife fell ill and died in 1986; and my daughter (then nearly fourteen) and I found ourselves picking up the threads of our rural life with only one pair of hands to keep it going. I am glad to say that it has kept going quite nicely.

Friendship with people native to the country and migrating into it, and professional work for quite a few of them, have therefore contributed substantially to the fund of information on which this book draws. So also has personal experience. But the total derives from events in the lives of hundreds of people; and while you might run into any of the problems discussed in the pages which follow (which is why they are there) you would find yourself in the *Guinness Book of Records* if you ran into all of them.

I hope, however, that the fact that they *are* there will prove fruitful in the fulfilment of your own objectives.

David Green
Castle Morris,
Pembrokeshire
1989

Chapter 1
Strategy and Tactics

Cottages in the country with thatched roofs and roses over the door have figured prominently in national nostalgia ever since destitution began to drive our ancestors off the land into the squalor of the early urban industrial revolution two centuries ago. But until very recent times the relative prosperity of urban living and the poverty of rural living which compelled that migration continued to prevent most people from making any significant attempt to reverse it. It was as if there was an unalterable rule: you can have a high standard of living in a city; or a high quality of life in the country; but unless you are already rich, you cannot have both. For the large majority, living in the country remained an unattainable dream.

Modern technology and communications are fast changing all that. More and more jobs can be done from virtually anywhere. Road, rail and air transport have eaten into the distances which separate people so that wherever you live it is possible to meet others, periodically at least, without too much difficulty. In between times computers and telecommunications allow ever increasing numbers to work together without being brought together. Never before has it been possible for so many people to live in the country and still retain urban living standards. Hardly surprisingly, given the steady erosion of city environments, more and more people are opting for country life, or are thinking of trying it.

There's a lot of country left

For most people the essential of country life is somewhere where there are open fields and landscapes. There are plenty of places left where that essential can be found. Our country extends over 94,000 square miles, but 46 million of its 56 million people live on no more than 24,000 square miles of that – in the rectangle with Liverpool, Hull, London and Southampton at its corners.

Most of the remainder occupy little more than another 1500 square miles; that's about all it takes to accommodate the cities of Exeter and Plymouth in the West Country; the Bristol–Newport–Cardiff–Swansea complex around the Severn estuary; the Newcastle–Durham–Stockton region of north east England; and the Glasgow–Edinburgh corridor in Scotland. So numerically, all but a tiny proportion of our people live on less than one-third of its land area.

Even within that one-third there are areas of open country. They are likely to stay that way as long as most of them are strictly controlled against further development by Green Belt and other planning policies and the same applies to open areas on their periphery. In all these stretches of open country, however, the way of life is already essentially urban. Houses in such convenient rural environments offer the easiest compromise between rural and urban living, and the amenity and convenience of existing property, and restrictions on further development, generate an insatiable demand for the housing stock which exists. Life in these areas is inevitably dominated by the towns and cities within easy reach, and by the lifestyles of the large numbers of people living in them who commute to towns and cities each day for work. Prices for property in such areas reflect the level of supply and demand: comparable properties almost always cost more than in adjacent urban areas.

That is only the state of play over about one-third of the country's total land surface. Beyond the urban and urbanised zones lie regions which become increasingly rural with remoteness and in which increasingly different conditions of rural living still predominate.

The transition between urban and rural living is far more gradual than the physical contrast between open land on the one hand and built-up land on the other may suggest. Because communications allow the influence of cities to spill out on a large scale, there is no sharp line dividing urban and rural ways of life, or distinguishing points where one ceases to dominate and the other takes over. The graduation between the two relates to distance, but more to distance measured in travelling time than in miles. In addition, as motor, rail and other communications reach out from city centres into remoter areas, corridors of urban living travel with them, though the greater the space between those corridors the more likely you are to find truly rural conditions surviving unchanged between them.

It follows, therefore, that however close you are to a built-up area, you begin to experience some of the differences – and some of the problems to which they give rise – if you move to any largely open area. The further you move, the more profound those differences are likely to become. And while long-established accessibility may have ironed out most of the differences in rural areas close to towns, accessibility may merely lull you into the false belief that urban norms endure in remote parts of the country which modern communications have only recently opened up. There accessibility may disguise more than it has changed.

These are things which it pays to bear in mind if you are setting out to discover a new rural home. As you distance yourself from town living your general experience will have less relevance to the things which you can expect in life, and it will become more important for you to sound out local realities in the area of your choice. As a simple example, when moving house in an urban area you may have been used to ringing up a plumber and arranging for him to be on hand to connect your appliances the day you move in and you may do the same in a deeply rural area. There, however, he may not turn up – immediately, for quite a long time after you make your move, or at all.

Even the remotest parts of the United Kingdom have become relatively accessible over the last 25 years and have begun to experience inward migration. Indeed, census returns show that some regions have their first positive increase in population for several centuries. But this new accessibility has not reduced the differences between rural and urban living to the superficial. And some new migrants, captivated overnight by a splendid house in a superb location at what often seems to be an unbelievably low price, have later found themselves ill prepared for the consequences. Quite a few have ended up facing real hardship though, like the pioneers which many of them are, most have managed to adapt over time and to survive.

Whether they have moved short or long distances, all these modern rural migrants have generated or contributed to a new body of experience. It is new because it is tailored to the realities of rural living in the latter part of the twentieth century. It is also new because, despite a short period of ill-informed idealism in the 1970s, when a handful thought they could turn all the laws of agricultural economics upside down by calling farming self-sufficiency, it has been inspired mainly by a conscious desire to achieve the best of all worlds – the high standard of urban living and the far more acceptable quality of country life.

Four fundamentals

Before turning to detail there are one or two generalities which might seem to be ludicrously obvious if so many people had not come a cropper because of one or other of them. They may indeed seem quite unimportant as you sit at home in a town house and plan how to make a break for the open country and where you might go, but they can become very important once you get there.

The climate

Large urban areas tend to iron out climatic extremes. Part of that process is entirely physical. The sheer quantity of heat which cities produce may take several degrees off the coldest weather; and the levels of atmospheric pollution which they generate may mask the most acceptable effects of the hottest and driest. Often only the most extreme weather conditions – like the hurricane which hit south east England in the autumn of 1987 – intrude significantly on city life. Where the weather does have impact the number of people on the ground allows public authorities to deploy small armies very quickly to clear away any obstacle to the smooth running of urban life which weather conditions have created. Even if the roads of a city should be piled 10 feet deep in snow, for example, it is inconceivable that they would be allowed to remain blocked for days, even weeks, afterwards. That is not so in remote areas where it can and does happen. So in cities the worst weather is never as significantly bad – and the best never as significantly good – as it may be once you are out in the open.

Before you start thinking about any move to the open country, therefore, you need to consider the sort of weather common in your chosen area round the year. If you will have to travel regularly you need to know if your communications are likely to be interrupted by floods, snow or damage caused by storms. And even if that risk does not present insuperable problems you should consider seriously your own tolerances and those of your family. Any location along the western seaboard of the United Kingdom is, for example, likely to experience significant periods of stormy weather and very heavy rainfall; any along the eastern seaboard may have periods of intense cold. Moreover, the more exposed the location you choose, the greater the impact on your life if they happen. There is a price attached to magnificent views over open sea or country: bad weather comes straight at you. So you need to consider very carefully whether these are things which you and your family can take in your stride, and that goes particularly for any members of it who may as a result be shut in at home for days on end, looking out on torrential rain and mud, and sometimes snow, without any measurable contact with others.

Population density

If you live in or close to any of the country's major urban areas your environment will contain on average at least 3000 people to the square mile. In the remotest areas there may be fewer than 200. All of us have an ill-defined, but deeply rooted, instinct for the number of people round us which leaves us feeling comfortable – the scale of our ideal community. In addition, each person's instinct of scale may be very different: ask any of your friends to give any example of a community which is an ideal size as far as they are concerned and you are likely to receive many different answers.

This instinct is subtly rooted. So deep does it run that when we are driven to live in vast communities with which we are totally uncomfortable we mentally subdivide them to an acceptable scale. We live in Hampstead, Highgate or Tower Hamlets, not in London. In Edgbaston or Sutton Coldfield rather than Birmingham. In Wilmslow, Withington or Prestwich rather than Manchester. In Milngavie – or perhaps the Gorbals – rather than Glasgow. It would defy anyone driving through or flying over these places to identify where they begin or end, but if we live in them we probably know their boundaries down to the last street.

The further out you go into the country the more the scale of communities seems to be defined merely by their physical extent. You may feel you can obtain a reasonable feel for Cambourne, Cardigan, Carlisle or Castle Douglas merely by looking at them. But even superficial appearances may be deceptive if you are looking at a place which attracts a large flow of holiday-makers each year, and you are looking at it, as so many of us do, during a holiday season. It is the level of activity generated by the indigenous inhabitants of a place which determines its year-long characteristics; and those characteristics are often not visible at all in periods when the local population may be doubled, trebled or more by vacationers. To acquire a reliable feel for most really remote places in the United Kingdom you have to visit in December, January or February, not June, July or August.

You should not underestimate the long-term importance, for you and your family, of choosing a location whose natural social scale leaves all of you feeling comfortable. Usually, anyone able to move to a chosen new location experiences a first flush of enthusiasm when the move is accomplished, particularly if the move involves a change as significant as moving from town to country. But if the scale of the community in your new location does not match a scale with which you and your family are content, the shortfall will very rapidly begin to erode the hopes and ambitions which prompted your move. And if any of you end up asking yourselves where all the people and shops are, having too few may quickly become as unsettling as having too many.

Your need to travel

The third fundamental is the extent to which your new location may create or increase your need for daily and other travel. The basic implications of commuting to work are fairly well understood by those who already do it; but while commuting presents no problems to some families and individuals, others find it exhausting, wasteful of their lives and increasingly corrosive of their relationships. If moving to the country means that some members of the family have a wonderful new life, while others spend all of theirs travelling or living out of suitcases, the unequal benefits can easily set up destructive tensions, particularly if the travelling members return home to scant concern for their weariness. If more commuting will be part of the price of your move to the country, you need to be very sure into which category you and your family fall.

The more remote the location you choose, the more lengthy daily or regular travel may become essential for your children if they are at school; and additional travel may be the only option for other members of your family if they are not content to spend long periods at home. Remoteness automatically eliminates both the easy access to shops, schools, clinics and other facilities which tends to be taken for granted elsewhere, and the social contact which goes with it. And while it will still be possible to find all these things by travelling to them, that implies a new burden on your family budget which can soon become substantial if it is frequently indulged. You and your family need to reflect carefully on how important those things may be to your sense of well being.

The impact on all of you

The emphasis on your family's feelings as well as your own is not laid accidentally. It is no use making a significant change in the way you are going to live if the result will impose stresses on you or other members of your family which may in the end fragment it. The unexpected hardships which some people have experienced after making a move to the country include the subsequent collapse of family relationships. Marriages have foundered because one partner could not stand the isolation, or another the change in career status. Children, particularly those who were teenagers when a family moved, have deserted back to the remembered vigour of adolescent city life as soon as they have had the opportunity. You all need similar levels of motivation and adaptability if it is to work. And if you have exchanged a house in an area where prices are geared to urban property price escalation for a remote house where they are not (and where they may only catch up when there is a surge in inward migration – perhaps years later), you need to remember that going back may quickly become financially impossible.

Finding your country area

None of these things proves insuperable for many people. You and your family may well be of their number. How then will you start your search? Many people who move to the country have already targeted a preferred area as a result of previous knowledge of it. But a good number start by looking first for likely locations on maps and that is not a bad way to begin. Even small-scale maps show the nature of the terrain, the open spaces which remain and indicate how remote you may be if you live in them – so long as they are up to date. If you then apply your own criteria and perhaps also those already discussed, you can take the planning process a stage further by eliminating areas which do not satisfy them and highlighting those which do. And since, as a general rule, the more remote houses are the less they cost, you may even be able to make some initial guesses as to where you will find somewhere you can afford.

Having pinpointed the region or regions which interest you, you can acquire the relevant 1:50,000 scale Ordnance Survey maps which give far more detail – even showing individual houses and hamlets in the open country. That will allow you to home in on specific locations where the ultimate and essential leg work on the ground comes into it.

Will laws governing property ownership matter?

The same or similar laws of property ownership and tenancy apply over most of the British Isles so in most places, whether inspired by original direct experience or the probabilities derived from maps, you can set about your search in the knowledge that the basic property rules you are accustomed to from urban life mostly still hold good.

There is, however, one important exception. In the remotest areas of Scotland – Orkney, Shetland, the Western Isles and the Highlands of Argyll, Inverness, Caithness and Sutherland – substantial tracts of land are subject also to the special jurisdiction of the Crofters Commission. Its offices are at 4–6 Castle Wynd, Inverness IV2 3EQ and some 17,700 crofts are registered with the Commission.

Highland crofts

Crofts are agricultural smallholdings, usually tenanted but sometimes owner occupied, and you cannot become the occupier of a croft without the consent of the Commission, even if the owner is willing to grant you a tenancy or an existing crofter is willing to transfer or sell you his. A crofter must, moreover, be permanently resident on and working his croft and the Commission can compel the re-letting of one which is vacant. No house or building forms part of any croft – they belong to the crofter who erects them.

Crofters may supplement their farm income with tourism and fish farming, and many do, for few crofts are sufficient on their own to provide a living; crofters may also compel their landlord to sell them their croft, though any croft so purchased remains subject to the Commission's rules and may not then be sold to (or, if sold, used by) anyone who is not approved as a crofter. It is possible to apply to the Commission for a declaration that a vacant croft shall cease to be such. But in considering such an application the Commission has regard to the general interest of the crofting community and to demand for crofting in the area. As the demand for crofts far exceeds the number which become available, crofts are not likely to be released from crofting control.

It follows, therefore, that before you commit yourself to any passion for the crofting areas, never mind any tenancy or purchase in them, reference to the Crofters Commission and to a lawyer in Scotland who knows the procedures is a vital first step. Without that you may discover, as some have, that you have paid for something which you cannot use and over which you have only vestigial rights.

Conclusions

Wherever you choose to start your search it is worth remembering a fundamental of human nature – it is far easier to be objective on general principles than it is on something specific. So it is much safer to look at a map, decide on an area which will meet your basic requirements, and then go out to look for a house in it, than it is to backtrack and try to give adequate weight to the realities of living in a particular area after you have already happened upon the house of your dreams there. The realities of life do not differ all that much between different houses in different urban areas where, if you find a house you fancy and you like its immediate environment, you can usually take everything else for granted. But in the country your first thoughts have to be for whether the *area* you favour is capable of delivering the things which you and your family consider essential; and the more remote it is the more specifically you have to question that. However enchanting houses may be, you cannot afterwards glue on to them infrastructures which are not there or climatic or other environmental conditions which are not natural to them. So you should only start looking for houses when you are satisfied that the area in which you are looking will meet your basic needs.

In principle, of course, there is no great difference from the approach which most people adopt when looking for urban houses. However, in an urban area the things for which you are looking usually consist of the visible hardware – what the houses, shops, schools and public services look like and where they are. You will still have to think about most of those things in the country in due course; but important things like remoteness, weather conditions, accessibility, how they may all interact, and how you and your family all feel about them, should come first and that is the difference. And since there are no obvious, easy or visible guides to these things, identifying the areas which are theoretically likely to meet your family's specific requirements, before you start any physical search for houses in them, may be a lot safer than starting with the house.

Checklist for homing in on your rural area

1. Is its year-round climate acceptable?
2. Are there enough people for your tastes outside holiday seasons?
3. Have you experience of it in January or February?
4. Will existing communications meet your travel needs, tolerances and budget? Are they vulnerable to interruption or closure?

5. Are its terrain, exposure to the weather, remoteness and natural features such that all of you can be happy?
6. If you are looking at the Highlands or Islands of Scotland, will you have to clear everything first with the Crofters Commission?

Chapter 2

The Cost of Living and Earning One

The commonest worry of those who want to move to the country is whether they can afford it. You are not likely to imagine that there is anywhere in the United Kingdom where you can step outside the money economy altogether, and if you do you will be swiftly disillusioned. But country living may also involve an entirely different financial ball game, and it is as well to be prepared for it.

The cost of rural living

Houses

The largest and most apparent item of expenditure will be your country house. You may strike lucky, but usually houses in country areas within easy commuting range of large centres of population cost more than comparable houses within those centres, even though local authority rates – and soon poll taxes – may be lower. By moving to such a house you will still have most, if not all, of the other facilities to which you are accustomed within reach and at the prices you are used to paying for them. But commuting costs will add a substantial surcharge. You may find that a smaller house in the country compensates in part for the cost differential but that is by no means guaranteed and at best is unlikely to cover all of it.

Many who have regarded a substantial promotion or salary increase, combined perhaps with a move to another area, as opening the door to country living have discovered this. Your family may love the idea of moving to a cottage in an Oxfordshire village, even if it is a third the size of your previous house and costs twice as much. But if your additional mortgage and commuting costs swallow all or more than the extra, and your daily commuting time extends from minutes to hours, you may all soon start wondering if it was worthwhile.

The further you move away from large centres of population the lower relative house prices are likely to be. There is a threshold beyond which you may be able to change between similar houses at less cost and this differential increases with distance until, in the remotest areas, houses may cost as little as a third of the price of their equivalents in high-cost regions like the south east of England.

Moving to such an area may make it possible for you to buy something larger with more land and facilities and still end up with money in the bank. But remember that there are always houses in any housing market which are overpriced in that market, and that you can easily fall for one of those if you are looking in an area where general price levels are lower than those to which you are accustomed. Taking out several months' postal subscription for the local newspapers circulating in your chosen area and studying all the housing advertisements in them is one way of attuning yourself to its normalities. Advice from local solicitors and estate agents may also prove valuable.

Other costs

Although remoteness may reduce house prices, it tends to increase virtually all other costs. The more remote an area, the less scope traders have for making a living by taking low profit margins from volume sales; and the more transport and the handling of broken bulk add to the cost of each item.

Admittedly, most of the national hypermarket chains have now established premises in the larger towns even in remote areas. So you may have a Tesco, Sainsbury or Marks & Spencer store, and their nationally determined prices, within feasible travelling distance of even the remotest location in England and Wales and of many in Scotland. But your own costs in travelling to reach such stores will add a heavy surcharge to their prices, so much indeed that you may find, if you analyse things carefully, that you still end up paying more for their goods than you would for those with a far higher price tag in your local shop. And there may be no way in which you can avoid the higher rural prices of goods which are not commonly available on a hypermarket basis

– petrol, consumer goods, building materials, technical services, and so on.

The impact of these differences is extremely difficult to quantify because it involves a few extra pence or pounds on each of the vast range of things which most of us use and need in the course of ordinary life. But the cumulative effect over years can easily absorb much, if not all, of the apparent advantage of lower house prices, particularly if in addition you plan to continue to commute regularly to an urban centre for work and are hostage to all the cost variables that involves.

Containing costs
There are, however, several things which you can do to contain this problem.

Minimise borrowing
Borrowing costs – interest and the like – are geared to the conditions which exist in urban life, to the levels of economic activity there and to all their fluctuations. The more you are exposed to these, the more your domestic economy is hostage to urban factors. If your country house is cheaper than your town one, take that as a warning that you are no longer in the urban pond, and that it is the generally lower level of incomes in the area surrounding you, and the higher level of other costs, which account for much of the difference. If your house costs a great deal less than your previous one, you may nevertheless share the popular belief that it is still sensible to borrow. If you do, however, abandon it. A mortgage might leave you with more free capital; but you'll be pretty lucky if, without risking it, you can make as much out of that capital as your mortgage interest will cost you. And if things do not go as well as you hope, each pound borrowed increases the risk to your whole new life.

Do it yourself
You need also to consider carefully how your abilities, energies and time will allow you to do things for yourself. The tools and equipment you choose may help you to win energy and time, and while their choice is likely to be as idiosyncratic to you as it is to everyone, the checklist of things which have proved useful in the country in Appendix 1 (pages 133–5) may help you. Any goods

or services which you can provide for yourself will save you the cost of buying them at current local prices – and probably of paying for them out of taxed income. If, for example, your rural house includes a substantial garden and perhaps other land, as it may well do, you can make a significant contribution to the cost of feeding yourself and your family by producing food from it – with the added advantage that you will know what has gone into your food and that it is fresh. This option is considered in greater detail in Chapter 4.

If you are a practical person you can eliminate substantial cost items by tackling yourself any of the jobs needing to be done on your new house usually carried out by the building trades. Some people who have bought semi-derelict houses in rural areas and who have done much of the restoration themselves have ended up with valuable houses at quite derisory cost. You may still have to pay more for building materials in a remote area than you would in an urban one – unless you can bring them with you – but labour contributes very substantially to building costs wherever they are incurred and while houses may be cheaper in remote areas building costs certainly are not. The general level of house prices in some remote areas is at times such that it is not possible to build new houses for comparable cost, which itself constrains new building in such areas.

As with your own food production there are other advantages in having building skills or acquiring them, even if by no more than trial and error. In remote areas you may have to hunt around for a long time before you can find anyone to carry out building work, and then have to wait an interminable time while they do it. Your chances of having things done when you need them are much improved if you can do them yourself.

Travel costs

The third aspect of rural cost cutting involves a very much more scrupulous regard for transport and travel costs – almost always by road in the country – than may have seemed necessary in any town. You may already be used to making only occasional visits to your local hypermarket, meat, freezer or town centre and to careful bulk buying of the large proportion of your household's regular needs on those visits. If you plan to live in the country, however, that may be the only way in which you can hope to retain the main part of the price advantage available in large trading establishments. In addition, it is almost always possible to cut hard into the costs of delivered supplies – solid fuel and oil, for example – by buying in quantities substantially larger than the urban norm.

If you do go in for irregular bulk buying, you will need more storage space at home than you are accustomed to, though the chances are that your rural house will provide it. A much larger deep freeze – 20 cubic feet or more for an average family perhaps – is often an essential component of the exercise, particularly if you are to grow some of your own food and will have seasonal surpluses which can be preserved for the leaner times of the year.

Again, cost is not the only consideration in planning for a far larger scale and range of household stores. Wherever you may be in open country, you may at times find yourself isolated from necessary supplies by anything from weather conditions to industrial disputes. As farmers of old long since realised if you always maintain back-up supplies in your own store, you don't find yourself in trouble if you can't get them out of someone else's.

Regular commuting for work, where it is unavoidable, creates by far the most significant part of the additional cost of travel which may follow a move to the country. Superficially, the least financially traumatic move to the country is one which allows you to retain your existing employment by travelling back to it each day, and hardly surprisingly hundreds of thousands of people do just that. But there are no guarantees on the future. You may weary of commuting, or your health or your family relationships may begin to crack up because of it and make it impossible. You may begin to think that you could make a far more constructive use of the time spent commuting: 'What is the point in spending all my life working like a fool in order to earn enough to pay others to do things which I could perfectly well do for myself if I was not working like a fool?'

Anything from another explosion in world energy prices to the closure of a rail line or withdrawal of a train or other transport service may throw a spanner in the works which totally changes all your economics. These things can happen, and they can make a real mess of all your country living if they do.

So, quite simply, if you aim to move to the country and

commute, you should include in your plans the prospect of finding work nearer home: and the greater the commuting distance the more urgently you should pursue it.

Earning a living in the country

What then are the options for living in the country *and* making a living there?

Telecommuting

While commuting has long been one way of transporting urban incomes into rural settings it is no longer the only one. More and more people, aided by computers, modems, telephone, fax and other devices (both existing and in the pipeline), are quite capable of delivering all that urban employments require of them without going anywhere near the delivery point, and with far lower overheads. Understandably perhaps, employers in information technology undertakings have been the quickest to realise this and the Xerox Corporation possibly leads the field. But the potential of modern electronics points increasingly to the opportunity for more and more people to use the whole of our country to its best advantage and you might well be able to exploit that potential.

So if the wish to move to the country grows larger in your mind, consider first whether it is possible to take all or a significant part of your job with you. How much of it in fact depends on your continuing to go in through a specific urban door at 9.00 am every working morning and come out of it at 5.00 pm? How much of your time which is capable of being productive is in fact lost because of the exigencies of travel and the growing chaos which accompanies it in urban areas? Is it actually necessary for you to be physically present at all those interminable meetings? How much of their business might be transacted with equal facility by telephone, fax and, when fibre optics shortly make it more widely possible, video communication? If you are in business on your own account, does your business really need to be where it is? Might it not be conducted at least as easily, and with far lower overheads, from where you would like to be? And if that is in a truly remote area are there government grants to help you move there and to keep you running when you arrive? There often are.

Many employers have never asked themselves these questions. After all, you are only asking them yourself because you want to move to the country and, at present at least, your employer does not. But if you analyse your work and can put up a persuasive case for being able to continue to do a significant part of it at least from a rural location, your employer may well be entirely receptive to the idea of telecommuting, particularly if you have special skills which are not easily replaced. And if your case is accepted you will be able to plan your move to the country free of any obligation for regular commuting and, whether you continue as an employee or become a self-employed subcontractor, with the part of your job that matters and its income tucked under your belt. The time you save may then be put to additional advantage.

Suppose that is not possible, and the only option is the traditional one of making your living from a location in the country. What are the odds?

Rural employment

People who live in rural areas do have jobs, though quality and quantity rarely meet demand. Local government is always a significant employer and central government may also be, particularly in the remotest areas to which military and defence establishments gravitate. The professions are always there – doctors, nurses, lawyers, accountants, architects, teachers and social workers. There are hauliers, bus companies, and railway employees if there is a railway. There are banks, building societies and insurance offices. If there is a sizeable port or harbour there will be port workers, maybe a port authority. There are shops and shop workers, builders and building workers. Almost always there are farms and farm workers. Frequently there is also a substantial tourist industry, catering for those who like the country but cannot, or do not choose to, live in it.

Rural employments governed by national conditions pay the same as they do anywhere, ignoring things like London weighting; but nationally remunerated jobs which include an obligation to move at the employer's behest offer no more long-term prospect of a settled existence in the country than they do anywhere else.

Once outside the net of local and national government and institutions, the level and value of local employment relate to the level and value of local business activity. And since the level and value is lower in rural areas, so generally is the reward. Professional people, for example, cannot usually hope to recover anything resembling the rates charged by their urban equals for the same work, though far lower overheads may redeem much of the disadvantage.

Basically, jobs in rural areas are not likely to pay as well as comparable ones in urban areas: and that is why this chapter first considers the cost of living in rural areas, and why you should also consider that carefully if you wish both to work there and preserve your accustomed standard of living.

Despite its lower level, the reward of rural employment is often a smaller problem than finding it. At best the number of rural jobs matches the scale of the existing population. There are fewer people, far fewer jobs and it is far more difficult to discover those which are available from outside. The rural bush telegraph functions very effectively and news of vacancies travels fast. Often someone is already known who can fill them and probably the majority of rural job vacancies are filled by people already living in the area. Many vacancies are never advertised at all and do not need to be; and many of those which are advertised only appear in local newspapers. Some professional and technical appointments may be signalled more widely but that is about all.

Other factors combine to compound the job seeker's problems. The turnover among people holding rural jobs is much less than is now common in more heavily populated regions. People tend to stay put. That may be very good news if you are a rural employer or intend to become one; but it is bad news if you want a job. There may well be very few new posts because there is no significant economic growth to create them.

The scale of rural businesses also enters into it. Lower levels of economic activity and slower or negligible growth in the volume of work to be done make for correspondingly smaller businesses and staffs. If an employer of 200 people takes on another it makes only fractional differences to his overheads; but the employer of two people faces a profound change in taking on a third. Because of their smaller scale rural professional, commercial and other businesses are far more cautious about employing more people. If they prosper they will first expect their existing staff to shoulder more and more of the additional work. They will tend only to recruit additions when everyone is so completely overloaded that even with another employee everyone will still be fully employed. This, incidentally, is something to remember if you believe that rural jobs are inevitably more relaxing and easy going.

You may still find a job you want through advertisement, local contacts if you have them, even local Jobcentres.

But if you want to carve out an employment niche for yourself in a rural area and are willing to shoulder some of the risks which you would normally expect others to assume, there is another possible approach. Arriving on the doorstep of a prospective employer or partner and asking for a job may well evoke short answers: 'We don't have one' or 'We can't afford another mouth to feed.' But if instead you present yourself as a self-employed person, dealing with your own accounts and overheads, and willing to offer such skill and time as a rural business can use, for a financial reward which relates specifically to the work you do, things may be different. If the business is overloaded with work, as many small rural businesses are, the chance to subcontract part of the overload may be attractive even if the price is half or more of the profit on the work let out. And if you are well qualified a rural business may think it a good bargain to have you under its belt. Ordinarily it might not have dared to recruit someone with your skills.

There are parallels to this approach in many occupations. Teachers may, for example, find it initially much easier to obtain supply or peripatetic teaching posts rather than full-time appointments in a rural area. But the consolation of achieving even a tenuous foothold is that once you have established working relationships it is a lot easier to evolve towards something more permanent. Moreover, once you are there within the employment market you have the same inside edge in it as other locals.

Finding a job in a rural area in the conventional way, or working yourself into one rather less conventionally, are therefore two of the alternatives if you cannot bring your income with you or do not want to.

A third is to acquire or start a business of your own.

Rural businesses
What sort of business?

You may have to wait for the opportunity but it is always possible to buy an established business if you have the resources – farm, shop, guesthouse, hotel or other undertaking.

Existing businesses
If you plan to buy an established business, make sure that you see full and complete accounts for it for several years before the date when you buy, and that those accounts are analysed for you by a skilled accountant if you do not have such skills yourself. Good businesses *are* sold in rural areas; but like rural jobs, and for similar reasons, they do not change hands very often. Unsuccessful or failing businesses are sold far more frequently and it will often only be the accounts which reveal in which category they fall. A business may be unsuccessful because the people selling it do not know what they are doing or because some trauma has affected the way they do it. Divorce seems to be a particularly common reason for the sale of small restaurants run by husband and wife teams, for example, though perhaps that in itself should be a warning. But lack of previous success may equally be the consequence of things which you cannot change – in the local business environment or changing economic conditions. It may quite simply be the wrong business, in the wrong place, at the wrong time. So if you plan to buy a limping business you need to be sure that you know why it is limping and that you can mend it.

If there is no inherent weakness in the trading prospects of a rural business you may well be able to continue the good work, but be very cautious even then about any business which depends heavily on the characteristics of its existing proprietors. In rural areas where everyone tends to know everyone else these things matter and news of any change travels fast. People's habit in continuing to patronise existing professional, commercial or trade premises tends to be more firmly rooted – which is a plus for your chances of inheriting someone else's goodwill in a premises-based business. But connections which are individual and personal may be far more fragile.

Alternatively, you may judge that you can start a new business from scratch. In that case, you are best placed if you are able to bring your existing business and its connections and goodwill with you.

Importing your existing business

There is almost always room in rural areas for entirely new businesses which cater mainly for the wider market outside and which bring some additional part of its wealth back. And just as the communications revolution has made it feasible for many people to continue doing urban work from remote locations, so it has also made it possible for businesses to take in their stride remoteness which might have been the kiss of death even 15 years ago.

Usually local councils and planning departments welcome anything which looks like bringing wealth and more permanent employment into a rural area; and the more remote a location, the more likely it is that government and other grants or allowances may be available to smooth the transition.

Specialised and high technology businesses seem to do particularly well in the country which often offers scientific instrument makers, electronic component manufacturers, computer software firms and most of the modern clean industries ideal conditions. Apart from space and naturally clean and attractive living and working conditions which may appeal particularly to skilled people brought in from outside, there is usually an untapped indigenous pool of people who want work and are untouched by the industrial habits conventional in traditional manufacturing regions.

Local labour may need training, but it will usually be diligent and well able to respond. In remote places in particular, the general level of ability and dedication is likely to be higher than in urban areas. The normal market for rural talent is limited and remote places have a long history of bright children with no choice but to leave in order to use their ability. But many of those children still prefer not to leave. So they and their children, passing in turn through the local schools, offer anyone setting up a new business better working raw material than they are now likely to find in most urban areas, and a far better chance of retaining it after it has been trained.

Finally, the factors which increase the cost of goods brought into rural areas for sale do not need to impinge in anything like the same way on businesses operating in and sending products out of them. If you run such a business you will, as you always do, plan your purchases to avoid the penalties generated when bulk is broken down through many hands. You will also plan the disposal of the goods you produce to make the most economical use of the transport which carries them.

Taking your business with you when you move into a rural area is therefore one way of taking your entire standard of living with you – and it may well prosper from your bargain.

Start from scratch

If you wish to start a new business in the country which will depend mainly on local rural trade, you should consider first whether it is entirely novel to that area or has competitors. If there are existing competitors you do at least know that there is a market for that type of business. And since, for the reasons already discussed, some of those competitors may be overloaded with work and consequently inefficient, you may have an initial built-in advantage: you will be seeking to collect enough work to keep you busy, they may be overloaded, and your starting service at least should be more efficient.

Once you have established your workload you will face exactly the same problem as your competitors – too much work, not enough hands or hours with which to do it, and the same worries about taking on any additional help. A professional man new to a rural area who faced that problem set about it entirely logically. He put a sign on his door saying that he would not accept any new business for three months, and did not suffer by doing so. But most people in that position are afraid to refuse work in case it might not be there when they want it again. That attitude, unless you have a very substantial staff, leads straight into the conventional problem of perpetual overload. If you start with an edge and want to keep it, you have to be resolute in controlling the volume of business you accept.

Businesses novel to the area

You may wish to start a business which is entirely novel to your rural area. If it is to depend on local patronage you have to consider carefully whether the absence of competitors merely signifies that there is no adequate demand. However, there is often room for outlets for entirely new things – witness the spectrum of computer-related businesses which have emerged in the countryside as they have everywhere else.

Tourist related businesses

A large number of the new businesses in rural areas – with or without existing competitors – are aimed at the travellers and tourists who bring some of the wealth of the wider market into them.

If you plan to go into any business which depends on tourism you must reflect very carefully on the multitude of trends which affect it. Tourists can come and go, for reasons quite unconnected with local conditions, including national economic trends considered in detail later on pages 37–9. And external factors may also influence the number of people aiming to get into the tourist industry very substantially.

Many people dream of owning a country pub, hotel or restaurant, for example. In periods when the value of urban houses has soared – as it did between 1971 and 1973 and has again between 1986 and 1989 – large numbers have found themselves suddenly sitting on vast paper cash surpluses. Many of them, particularly those who have been quick off the mark before urban property price inflation has penetrated rural and remote areas, have decided that the time has arrived to fulfil their rural dream. They have realised previously unimagined wealth by the sale of their urban houses and ploughed it into country hotels, pubs or restaurants. So much so in recent times that the number of new hotels and similar premises opened in the period 1986–1988 has reached record levels.

Sadly, many of them will not survive – particularly those who have also needed to borrow to indulge in substantial improvements and alterations. The trend which brings them into the countryside is not one which will increase the value of the tourist trade on which they will then depend. Indeed, if that trend is corrected by raising interest rates, the trade may reduce.

Now to some specifics.

Hotels, guesthouses, self-catering premises and their agency management

In many rural areas the traditional holiday was taken in hotels by a small number, and in guesthouses – including farms – by the majority. Substantial numbers also opted for self-catering holidays, mostly in caravans. The caravans remain, though sites and numbers are now strictly controlled by the planning authorities (see Chapter 7 if you are interested in acquiring an existing site – and beware of your chances of ever being allowed to start a new one). Hotels have benefited from a modest growth in demand. But guesthouses, whether providing full or partial board, are in steep decline and the preference increasingly is for houses equipped and furnished to the highest standards and let for self-catering.

The overhead costs of providing hotel and high standard self-catering accommodation are materially higher than those of guesthouses (where fewer rooms may also do double duty as the proprietor's home), and far higher than those of caravans. So hotels and self-catering properties have to function well outside conventional holiday periods if they are to operate economically.

Many rural hotels have tackled this problem by investing heavily in additional facilities – squash courts, indoor swimming pools, conference and function centres, and so on – to attract a greater volume of trade in all seasons from both local and distant origins, and in the advertising necessary to make their facilities known. Most owners of self-catering properties now have their properties managed and advertised by one or other of the many groups of large-scale self-catering property promoters which have sprung up to meet the need and to cut the heavy cost of individual advertising. It is far easier to guarantee and advertise objectively the standard and nature of large numbers of properties than to cope with the variables of catering in guesthouses; and, apart from the underlying change in public taste, the difficulty of group advertising for the latter has contributed to their decline.

If, therefore, you plan to become an hotelier you need to research the whole field carefully, and almost certainly need previous hotel experience. If you plan to start or operate a guesthouse, you need to be very cautious indeed, for most of the guesthouses which are now likely to flourish are those which offer special additional attractions – farm guesthouses with fishing, pony trekking or special farm interests, for example. If you intend to offer self-catering property you need to be sure that it is not already oversubscribed in your local market. Almost certainly you should place the management of your property in the hands of one of the large local or national businesses which now advertise such property. They may charge you 20 per cent or more of all your rental income for the privilege. That might prompt you to consider whether starting such a business yourself would be worthwhile – it might if the available property in your chosen locality is not already largely committed. But, however it may be, only substantial national advertising is likely to guarantee that your property is occupied all the year round; only year-round occupation, which usually compensates for the high cost of agency management, is likely to show a significant profit from self-catering property.

Pubs

Country pubs are vulnerable to the increasing tightening of controls governing drink and driving. Many rural pubs already depend very much on the limited trade available in their immediate locality. Planning consent and Justices' licences for new pubs are not easy to obtain, though there is usually no great difficulty in obtaining a restaurant or residential licence to sell alcohol. So, almost inevitably, if you want to run a pub, you will have to become the tenant or owner of one which already exists. In rural areas close to major centres of population you may well be able to improve on existing trade by offering additional and better facilities; you may be able to do the same in remoter areas though there your gain will almost inevitably be your competitors' loss, if the trade available overall remains the same. The accounts of an existing pub are, as with all existing businesses, a vital area of study. But if you hope for growth in a remote area you must also look very closely at all your competitors. There are cases, surprising though it may seem, where newcomers have, for example, added a proudly proclaimed restaurant to their pub, in total ignorance of the fact that there was another one only a mile down the road with the best local reputation for 30 miles in any direction. They failed.

Timeshare properties

A timesharing development may yield huge profits if it is done well. If the scheme is linked to one of the international agencies which allow timesharers to exchange their designated weeks with others – as most are – it will be additionally attractive. But the technical difficulties in setting up a timeshare scheme are enormous. The property law of the United Kingdom does not acknowledge the existence of a timesharer's interest, and making that interest convincing and marketable is therefore a formidable legal undertaking. The market for timeshares is also limited and that market has shrunk as news of badly established schemes and schemes (mainly abroad) – which have sometimes been entirely fraudulent – has spread. The promotion of a timesharing scheme is not something to contemplate without extensive and costly professional, technical, marketing and financial advice.

General tourist attractions

Modern tourists expect a great deal more of any area which they visit than merely its natural scenery and many businesses which cater for this voracious taste for variety now flourish in rural areas. Farms which have diversified into interesting and more profitable activities – making cheese or ice cream, rearing and working heavy horses or rearing exotic or unusual animals – have found that they can profit additionally by admitting and charging visitors who want to see what they are doing. Artists and craftsmen have always tended to proliferate in rural areas with low overheads and if you are a painter, sculptor, potter, woodworker, leather or metal worker you may be able to make a living from your art or craft in a rural area to which tourists come, even if you are not able to sell anything anywhere else. In addition, if there are enough artists and craftsmen in your area you may be able to make a living by providing them with services: picture framing for the painters, or galleries displaying and selling their work.

Things which are entirely novel to a locality may also do well – rare breed collections if there are none, butterfly farms rearing and displaying exotic tropical insects, fresh water or ocean aquaria, leisure parks and activity centres. Such specialities may all prosper and have prospered in appropriate locations. But brave new ventures in a rural area will only attract tourist patronage if they are well done for, as ever in the country, bad news will travel fast. You have to know your market, your speciality and have adequate finance to indulge it if you aim for real novelty.

Farms and farm-related businesses

Farming, and sometimes fish farming and forestry, is still a mainstream activity in most rural places. If you have the skills which farming needs and the very substantial capital which it requires, you can still hope to make a reasonable living as a farmer, though you should remember that you will need several hundred acres of land to do it by conventional methods. If you can devise means for bringing back over your farm gate far more profit than is to be made by the conventional production and sale of general farm produce, you may be able to make a reasonable living with far less land and capital. Some of those who have added cheese, ice cream, yoghurt or other manufacture to ordinary milk production have been able to do that because the price their finished product will command may be three, five or ten times as great as that which the Milk Marketing Board would pay for their milk – with very limited additional capital, labour and material cost. Some of those producing to meet the growing demand for organic produce have also done well on limited resources because of the higher premiums which such produce commands.

But remember that quotas bite increasingly into the things which any farmer can do with his land. For example, you may not now produce potatoes or cows' milk commercially unless you have a quota which covers your production. Admittedly, the milk from goats and sheep is not so controlled, so if you know what you are doing with goats and sheep you can produce their milk and its products. But whatever you produce you should appreciate that you will be subject to increasingly stringent public health and disease control standards, that complying with these costs money, and that that cost alone may in the end destroy the possibility of profit from smallholdings which were quite capable of substantial profit before everyone heard about salmonella and listeria.

Like every other major economic activity farming has an infrastructure of trades which support it. As farms become ever larger they increasingly furnish themselves with all the plant and equipment which they are likely to need. But independent contractors – ploughing, seeding, crop spraying, fertilising and harvesting, for example – are still in demand in some places and are likely to remain so. So if your interest lies in farm contracting or machinery maintenance, there may yet be a niche for you in a rural area – though you will need to research the possibility with particular care and will require substantial financial resources if you plan to acquire farm machinery.

Borrowing for rural businesses

The way in which attitudes to borrowing may need to be different in the country has already surfaced in the discussion of rural houses (see page 22). No apology is given for returning again to the theme in the context of rural businesses where it is even more significant.

In any business which depends mainly on the patronage of people living in a rural area, and many others (particularly those where trade fluctuates with the seasons and where periods of low activity have to be financed), it is far more important than it may be in an urban area to have adequate financial resources of your own, and not to rely any more than you can help on borrowing. When people buy or start businesses in cities they often do not seem to think twice about going to the bank and borrowing as much as they can, but that logic often leads to disaster in the country.

You may well be able to borrow the money you want – you may not need as much capital as a city business and your house alone will often be sufficient security. But if you start that way you may have a very painful ride.

You have to remember, as you do with rural houses, that the interest on borrowed money is the same wherever you borrow it. The rates are geared to the conditions which exist in the national financial market and that, overwhelmingly, is the urban market. In rural areas you are most unlikely to be able to generate the volume, and often the regular frequency of trade, which matches that available in an urban area. Interest is therefore always likely to take a larger slice of your earnings than in a comparable urban business. And even if conditions look good when you take up your borrowing, minor shifts in national financial conditions can make major differences to the more fragile economy of remoter areas.

Farming and tourism have supplied some particularly painful examples of what can happen, and how it can happen, during the last decade. Through most of the 1970s rates of inflation outstripped levels of bank interest; in addition, the increase in the nominal values of the properties against whose security people borrowed exceeded inflation. With security which was apparently entirely adequate, and growing in value as well, and with sums borrowed therefore shrinking daily as a proportion of the total value of the assets on which they were secured, people borrowed heavily and banks were more than willing to lend.

Meantime, also responding to inflation, the external exchange rate for the pound fell. Relatively, imported food was more expensive than home-produced food and farms prospered. That in turn further boosted prices for farmland, particularly when large investors entered the market to hedge their funds against inflation. That seemed a very safe bet when every purchase which they made still further increased the value of what they had bought. As one farmer put it: 'Buy land, my boy. They aren't making any more.'

The same economic conditions produced a massive increase in domestic tourist traffic. With the low pound, holidays in the United Kingdom became, relatively, very cheap. People from all over Europe swelled a growing number of British holiday-makers. The returns from, and value of, tourist businesses soared and people running them borrowed heavily to invest for further profit.

In rural areas, particularly the remotest, agriculture and tourism enjoyed an unprecedented bonanza.

Then all that changed, almost overnight. The government decided to halt inflation. Interest rates were the chosen instrument for that exercise and they were raised to levels which ensured that lenders had a positive return over and above the rate of inflation.

This immediately imposed a substantial real cost on borrowers. The exchange rate of the pound rose as foreigners bought for the better interest offered, foreign food became cheaper and home-produced food more expensive, farm profits began to dwindle and farm and land prices began to fall. Institutional investors began to pull their investments out of farmland and move their money into more rewarding investments. The price of farms and farmland fell still further. Then it collapsed altogether for a while when the EC started to eliminate surplus food production by imposing national quotas.

Tourism had a similar experience. As the pound rose, British holiday-makers found that they could buy continental holidays with guaranteed sunshine far more cheaply than the often wet ones they had taken in the United Kingdom the year before. Foreign holiday-makers made the same discovery and the tourists disappeared within a season. Farms and tourist businesses which had borrowed heavily found themselves in the same hole. They could not earn enough to pay the higher bank interest; and, in a market in which suddenly everyone was trying to sell, they could not sell out for enough even to repay their borrowing. Many became bankrupt.

The ones who survived were those who had not delivered themselves as hostages to lending institutions by heavy borrowing and were able to batten down the hatches and ride out the storm. For the survivors, and now again newcomers to the market, these particular traumas are behind us and the value of businesses affected by them has largely returned to its previous level. That, however, has not saved those who became bankrupt in the meantime.

Such shifts in national priorities can occur again – and again. The moral therefore is quite simple. If you want to make a total break from urban living, try not to leave yourself hogtied to its economic conditions with any borrowing beyond that which is absolutely essential. And if you want to invest in growth in your rural business, feel your way forward slowly and carefully with ploughed-back profits, rather than precipitately with massive loans.

Conclusions

With diligence and perhaps a little luck you should be able to find yourself a source of rural income as well as a rural home if you try – particularly if you have special knowledge, experience or training honed by your urban years. That source may be different, may not sound as important, and may not yield as much as your town job did. But if your move to the country allows you to buy more house for less cash; your rural job makes it possible to save the money and time which you previously frittered away in commuting; and if in particular you choose to apply spare time and energy to producing things for yourself and your family which you would otherwise have to buy, you may all be better off in the country than in the town in every sense of the words. Burning energy – and keeping fit – by producing things may not have the glamour of burning the same energy by jogging, or playing squash, golf or any other sport (most of which will still be available to you if you want them anyway), but it does add pluses to your domestic economy rather than minuses. Ultimately it is not the number of zeroes after the figures on your pay cheque which matter, but whether the figures in it are larger or smaller than the cost of the things you need and want to buy. Conventionally the route to those is to earn more money; but needing to spend less money may be equally effective.

Checklist for the economics of your plans

1. Will the changes in your housing and other costs leave your family budget with a net gain or loss?
2. Can you win acceptable (and if need be sufficient) economies by limiting borrowing and travelling requirements? Can you economise by doing things for yourselves? (See also the checklist in Appendix 1 for DIY tools and equipment.)
3. Will your income change? Can you sustain it by telecommuting, commuting (after allowing for commuting costs) or bringing your town business with you?
4. Have you explored employment prospects in your chosen area?
5. Do you plan to go into business in that area? If so, have you researched exhaustively any existing business you plan to buy, or the prospects of, and existing competition for, any new business you plan to start?
6. Have you allowed for the additional vulnerability to borrowing costs of businesses in remote areas?

Chapter 3
Country Houses

In urban areas everything is usually cut and dried and well tested over time. Urban houses change hands more often than country houses and under historic conveyancing practice everything has been investigated over and over again each time a change has occurred. Houses are built of bricks and mortar; they have well established and defined boundaries, access roads, water supplies, sewers, gas, electricity and telephone services; your land is clearly and exclusively yours and your neighbour's theirs. The same is likely to apply if you buy a modern house in the country. But the chances are that you won't.

The proportion of old houses is larger in the country. And often country houses are only sold because someone who has lived in them for years has died; or because they have become redundant to farming or other local use as the result of a farm amalgamation, a decline in the indigenous population, or a move by their previous occupants into modern accommodation. And in any event many people want an old house.

Old houses can be a very different kettle of fish.

The fabric of old houses

The differences may start with the fabric. Most often old houses were built to styles evolved in the locality with whatever materials were readily available in it. They may be built of bricks and mortar and have slate roofs. But they may not. Many cottages in the West Country are built of cob – a mixture of clay, gravel and straw. Originally they probably had thatched roofs and they may still have them. Those which survive may have stood there for several hundreds of years and there is nothing unenduring about them so long as the roof remains sound and water does not find its way into the walls. But if you charge in and buy a beautiful white limewashed cottage, you may face some cultural shock if you then discover that effectively there is a mud hut concealed within it; and you certainly have to be thoughtful about alterations if there is.

If houses are built of stone, as many are in the rocky areas of the country, the stone may be squared (ashlar) in which case the chances are that the fabric is essentially the same as bricks and mortar with the stone substituting for brick. But if the stone is natural random stone of all sizes – and the thicker the walls the more likely this is – it is probable that the house was built with the flattest and most regular surface of each stone on the outer faces of the walls, and that the irregular parts were then bonded together with a mixture of smaller stones, stone rubble, clay and lime (mud again) in the middle. Any mortar visible probably only points the gaps between the stones on the outer face and does not go very far into the wall at all.

Nevertheless such houses also endure indefinitely so long as the roof remains sound and water does not penetrate the walls, loosening the original bonding; and so long as the bonding is not shattered by subsidence or vibration, most commonly these days from traffic. If that happens, however, the inner and outer faces may begin to peel apart, and sooner or later the whole wall may come down.

Alterations to such houses can also be tricky. You can bring a whole random rubble wall down by knocking a few holes in it and such walls require careful propping beforehand. You may find that the fabric includes vast boulders and that you end up having to rebuild large parts of the house if you merely want to put a small window in. If the stone is granite, dolerite or some other very hard rock, you can also face real problems if you need to drill a small hole in the wall to fix something.

In chalky areas of the country like Hampshire and the Isle of Wight many houses survive in which flint was the main building material. Again this may be locked together with anything from mortar to clay and again there is no real problem with flint walls unless or until they have been disturbed or you find yourself wanting to drill a hole in them.

Half timbering with thatch or tiles for the roof is the main vernacular method of house building to have survived over much of central England. However, half timbered houses may be found anywhere, for the method of construction was widely used, and those which survive often say more about local exposure to wind and rain than anything else.

Most half timbered houses have a massive prefabricated frame, usually oak, and originally at least had wattle and daub panels filling the spaces between the frame members. The wattle consisted of twigs woven into basket-like panels and the daub most often a mixture of cow dung, animal hair, clay or plaster. Many survive in that condition and their outward appearance usually declares the fact. However, wattle and daub can decay and you may well find half timbered houses with panels of brick either original or built in as replacement. Their essential fabric is also clearly visible. The main need for caution arises with half timbered houses whose fabric has been buried in subsequent brick or rendered facings. That may have been done to cover decay which existed; but burying timber in masonry may also cause or accelerate decay.

Building work on old houses

Replacing the vast timbers in half timbered houses demands skills now possessed by a handful of craftsmen only, and involves a fearful expenditure on materials and time. Since many half timbered houses are also listed buildings, protected against alteration, it is not likely to profit you greatly if you buy one which needs substantial repair or alteration.

In general, modern building regulations and costs combine to prevent many traditional building materials from being used in new houses. But in areas containing vernacular buildings there are usually builders experienced in dealing with the problems to which they give rise, and the greater the proportion of such buildings, the more any local builder is likely to have the requisite skills in his armoury.

Surveys before you buy

If you require a mortgage to finance your purchase, your building society or bank will almost always insist that the property be valued by its valuer. It used to be thought that such valuations gave you no protection since they were commissioned by and for the lending agency and in any event were intended to reveal the market value of the property and not necessarily defects in it. Such valuations were therefore far cheaper than the full surveys which purchasers commissioned for their own advice; and while such surveys gave purchasers the right to claim compensation if something significant was missed through negligence, less than a third of purchasers were willing to pay the price.

Our final court of appeal – the House of Lords – has now ruled that if a building society valuer misses something through negligence the house purchaser can claim compensation from him. Much of the difference between having your own survey and relying on a building society valuer may therefore have disappeared, though if it has building society valuations will probably rise in cost to or towards the level of your own survey.

Be that as it may, the older the house, the more likely it is that it may contain some serious defect and the more important it is to investigate its condition. Unless you are prepared to take things on chance by judging them yourself, and unless you have the resources to deal with anything really nasty which turns up, you will be wise to commission and pay for a full survey of an old house even if no bank or building society insists upon one. But whether you do it yourself or pay to have it done, no survey can or will reveal things which could only be discovered by taking a house to pieces, and people offering to sell you a house are not likely to allow that. To that extent, therefore, even surveys will be qualified and will not protect you if they are.

In any event your life is likely to be a lot easier if your own eye is tuned in to some of the things which anyone should look for. If you have a surveyor and he does his job properly and lists every defect which can be discovered, you are still likely to have to judge how important some of them really are. And if he fails to do his job and you end up with the chaos of unexpected building work, the cost, worry and delay of recovering damages against your surveyor are likely to be poor compensation, particularly if you have to fight it through the courts.

With or without a surveyor, therefore, it helps to be able to look at your country house through eyes which are part open at least. Most of this chapter deals with things that may profit from consideration and there is a checklist in Appendix 2 which may also be helpful.

How important are basic appearances?

We all have an instinct for tidiness and, so far as can be seen from their relics, the same applied to our ancestors right back into the mists of time. However old a house may be, the chances are that the man who built it built walls which were straight, vertical and with a regular face, whatever materials he used; his roof faces would be flat and even and his roof ridges horizontal; and his chimneys would be square to the house and would not twist, bend or bulge unless obviously designed to do it. If the walls, roofs and chimneys still look like that when you come to consider his handiwork, it suggests fairly strongly that nothing has moved in the meantime and that the basic fabric – which is the thing which really costs money if anything is wrong – remains as sound as it was when the house was first built.

If, however, any of the walls bulge, lean or have cracks running up through them; or if the chimneys do the same or have weeds growing out of them; or if the roof surface looks as if it has been breathing in and out; or its ridge lines are like a switchback; or gaps exist in or between slates or tiles, the chances are that something has moved and may still be moving. All buildings tend to settle a little over time, not all roof ridges were built with timber which allowed them to be entirely horizontal, and minor changes in shape may not have impaired stability. But if walls, roofs or chimneys are cracked or have changed shape or direction you need to establish the underlying cause. The state of the roof may indicate anything from rusting slate nails to rotting timbers – a look inside the roof should quickly give the answer. Eccentric chimneys may need an expensive rebuild. Eccentric walls may indicate subsidence, inadequate strength to resist outward floor and roof pressures, or disintegration of the bonding even of the basic material. Remedying any of these costs real money.

What you may find anyway

Damp

You can expect some damp and some sign of woodworm in most old houses. If a really old house is still there at all, the chances are that it will not have made any great difference to it and will not make much difference to you either. Vernacular builders did not have to calculate the strengths and tolerances of their materials down to the last millimetre as modern builders do. So the strength of the walls and timbers in old houses was often vastly greater than required by the structure and such walls and timbers may tolerate a considerable degree of decay and attrition without creating any weakness.

In any event, damp does not necessarily rise osmotically through some building materials as it does through brick, and old builders knew some of its risks and often built to avoid them. In brick-built houses a couple of courses of hard blue engineering brick may substitute entirely adequately for a bitumen or other impervious membrane, and be better than a wall which slips slightly and breaks a membrane. Half timbered houses usually had their base timbers laid on large sandstone or other stone blocks to protect them. But whether or not there is any apparent damp course, you should always be careful if an old house has hollow wooden floors at ground level (ie boards, not parquet surfaces on a solid base); or if the land outside is above internal ground-floor level. Hollow wooden ground floors are very vulnerable to rot in old houses and, whether or not there is a damp course for it to bridge, any build-up of soil against an outer wall will lift the level of damp in the wall, hazarding upper floors.

Rotten timber

You can expect some rotten timber in an old house. Wet rot may not matter much since it will only damage the timber visibly affected, though it is wise to try and eliminate the source of the water which causes it. Dry rot will, however, march through everything and lock itself into walls as well. Dry rot is only likely to be halted and cured by cutting out and replacing all affected timber, hacking off plaster on all affected walls and by treating everything with appropriate chemicals. But if its cilia have rooted themselves deep into walls demolition and rebuilding may be necessary to stop it. Inevitably it often proves very costly to cure dry rot, particularly if yours travels into your neighbour's adjoining terraced or semi-detached house and you have to pay for his as well. If you intend to be your own surveyor you should research dry rot in detail if you cannot otherwise recognise it. Beware anyway if you find timber whose surface is cracked into a mosaic pattern and crumbles under pressure; or fungus fruit bodies growing out of it anywhere.

There are several modern answers to rising damp. They include injecting silicones or inserting specialised ceramic tubes into walls, as well as electro-osmotic cures designed to lead back to earth the electric potential which is understood to contribute to the rising damp phenomenon. There are also cures for penetrating damp: repointing is the traditional and often the most effective answer, though rendering with or without pebble dash, and hanging slates or tiles on walls are also old favourites. Modern silicone and textured and other sprayed paints may be at least as effective. So if you want a house entirely free of damp, or if damp presents a significant risk to the fabric of your house, you will almost certainly be able to buy an appropriate remedy from one of the contractors who offers it. If you rely on a mortgage for your house, the lender may insist that you do that anyway. But people have lived in houses with some damp quite happily for centuries so do not imagine that all damp necessarily demands attention and expense.

Woodworm

Ordinary woodworm (the larva of the beetle *Anobium punctatum*) may not imply any great hazard to the fabric of an old building. It prefers sapwood and unseasoned wood, and though old floorboards may be pulverised, both the size and seasoning of the main timbers used in old houses is likely to ensure that even if woodworm has attacked there will be plenty of strength left. However, lath and plaster partition walls may be more vulnerable, particularly if those who constructed their hidden sub-frames used convenient branches taken straight off trees, often not shaped at all from their original form. Modern chemical treatment of timber attacked by woodworm is usually effective and several proprietary liquids, also effective against rot, are available from builders merchants. You may well be able to paint or spray your timber yourself – unless your building society or other lender demands a professional certificate and guarantee. If you have to put any new timber into any part of your house, it should be systematically treated: rarely if ever is modern timber either seasoned or of a quality to resist damp or woodworm. The existing fabric of your house may be such that treatment is not essential, but as the woodworm beetle is always around and as it can also wreak havoc with your furniture, limiting its opportunities is always wise.

The larva of death watch beetle (*Xestobium rufovillosum*) is far rarer and far more damaging. It may attack any old wood, causing havoc. If you are your own surveyor you need to be able to spot the differences, and to carry out a minute and detailed examination if death watch beetle is present.

Mice and other rodents
Rodents – mice and sometimes rats or grey squirrels – may be your other pest problem, particularly if the fabric of your building contains natural voids which most old houses do. Rodents may be permanent residents; more frequently they will merely find their way into your house from surrounding fields in the autumn and leave it again in the spring. If this is the case they are likely to have long-established pathways through the fabric of the building, some of which may come to light if you have to burrow into old walls. Rodents inevitably pose some health hazard if they can get near your food, and they will help themselves to any accessible animal food. They may also try to drink water out of the cold water storage tanks in your roof or elsewhere, particularly in dry weather. Some will probably fall in, drown themselves and then decompose. You and your family probably know already that water which comes through such storage tanks, usually through the hot water taps, should never be drunk, but the prospect of drinking the essence of a decaying rodent should highlight the message. Floating corpses in a storage tank may also explain developing foul smells in your hot water supply.

The main hazard of rodents is, however, not dirt or disease but the voracious appetite they have developed for the plastic sheathing on electric cables in universal use now for several decades. Exposed cables in your roof, under your floors, in your outbuildings and particularly in any warm place where mice may congregate, may be eaten bare so that they short-circuit and cause a serious fire risk. Most old houses are stuffed with dry timber and other combustible material and it can be very difficult to stop a fire once it has started. It is, therefore, as important to keep rodents at bay after you buy as it is to have a detailed check of any existing wiring which is to be retained beforehand. It may pay to have traps permanently baited and set in warm places like airing cupboards and to ask your local Environmental Health Officer to send someone in periodically to lay down poison.

Listed buildings, conservation areas, and houses long unoccupied

If your rural house is in a conservation area or is listed as having architectural or historic interest, there may be strict planning controls on any change or alteration. If it has been long unoccupied the right even to use it as a house may have been abandoned under planning law; and even its use as a house, never mind substantial alterations, may require planning consent and building regulation approval. These issues may affect your plans; they may also affect you indirectly if a previous owner has done something without proper approval. They are considered in greater detail in Chapter 7.

Improvement grants

Improvement grants may be available for houses built before October 1961 and they may also cover repairs to houses built before 1919. At present grant funds are rationed. After 1990 they will also be means-tested and that may disqualify many people who can afford to buy a rural house. In any event, you may have to wait some time for grant approval and as grants must be fully approved before any building work starts, submission of a grant application should have high priority. Grants are available for owner occupied and tenanted houses, but not for holiday and second homes or commercial developments. However, tourist boards and development agencies may have funds available for tourist projects. Local councils and relevant boards or agencies can supply details.

Important rights, services and obligations

Rural houses often pose problems of detail, many of which are likely to be raised and resolved if you have a solicitor acting for you before you start buying. But sometimes the fact that questions need to be asked is only revealed by seeing a house and since solicitors dealing with conveyancing rarely do that it is as well to be on your guard.

Boundaries

If the boundaries of your house and land are clear and obviously long established you probably have no problems. But if there are gaps in them those gaps may indicate that someone else has a right of way through your property; if the boundaries are open you need to have them clearly defined before you commit yourself.

Unless the deeds of your property say otherwise any boundary which consists of a hedge, whether or not it be on a bank, is likely to run down the centre line of the hedge and bank. But if there is a bank with a ditch on either side of it the law will assume that whoever dug the ditch dug it on the boundary of his own land and threw the soil from it back to form the embankment inside his land. So your side of the ditch may be the boundary if it is on your side of a bank, and his side of it if it is on his. Unfortunately, even that is not guaranteed for long-established subsequent practice may have changed the position. If someone has cleared and maintained the ditch for more than 12 years the ditch may be his, and if he has erected a fence outside that period the fence may mark the boundary.

If you have a fence on your boundary the law will assume that whoever erected the fence planted the posts on the boundary so that he could then nail the rails or wire on to it from his own land: the posts therefore mark the boundary. If you have a river or stream on your boundary, usually the boundary will run down the centre line of the stream – and will change its position with any natural change in the course of the stream.

If your land is higher than your neighbour's you may be legally liable to him if lumps of yours fall on to his. If you have trees growing on your land and their roots spread causing damage on his you may also be liable. If trees on your land overhang your neighbour's boundary he can remove the overhanging branches. All these things apply both ways, of course (see Chapter 8 dealing with nuisance).

Boundaries, disputes relating to them, and rights over other people's land generate more rows than virtually anything else so be very careful that you do not start a feud with your neighbours or inherit one when you buy.

Rights of light

Rights of light can only be acquired through defined windows and similar apertures but include the right to enough light to grow plants in long-established greenhouses. If not specifically provided for in your deeds, rights of light will normally be established to any aperture which has been there unobstructed for more than 20 years and once established they can be protected against any deliberate obstruction which materially reduces the light coming in – new buildings but not things like the natural growth of trees. You do not now have to erect an obstruction to prevent your neighbour acquiring a right of light through a new window and you might in any event have to obtain planning permission before you did. You can instead register a protective notice under the 1959 Rights of Light Act.

Rights of way

Rights of way may go with your rural house; other people may enjoy such rights over it (see also Chapter 6).

General public rights of way exist over public highways, footpaths and bridlepaths – the existence of the last two being dependent on whether or not they are shown on the maps and described in the schedules originally prepared under the National Parks and Access to the Countryside Act 1949 and maintained under subsequent legislation. Local district and sometimes National Park authorities keep and can supply the details. The fact that a track or route is shown on an Ordnance Survey map, however, merely means that it exists. It does not mean that there is necessarily any public or other right over it.

Private rights of way, the benefit of which is attached to specific properties, also exist. They may be created specifically by deed; they may be implied by law if someone sells property with an existing access, or if it can only be reached over land which he retains. Like public rights of way, private rights may come into existence if someone uses the route openly, apparently and without permission; but while there is no minimum period of use necessary to the creation of a public right, anyone asserting a private right must be able to show that they have used the route for at least 20 years.

But rights of way over someone else's land are rights to pass and repass only along the established route. They do not include the right to park on the route, obstruct it, wander about away from it, or reconstruct, widen or improve it. And they do not include the right to use it for any purpose beyond that for which it was originally granted or created. So you cannot take horses or vehicles down a footpath; you cannot take vehicles down a bridlepath; and you cannot use a right of way granted for agricultural purposes for any other purpose. If your country house fronts on to a public highway, your only significant problem is likely to be whether anyone else has rights of way over your land. But if access to it lies over an unmade road, or relies on a private right of way, you need to be sure that you have the rights to use it, that the extent of the use suffices for all your purposes, and that there is no history of previous disputes about any of these things.

Water supplies

You have to have water. If your country house is connected to the main water supply you face no great problem, though if the supply is metered you are likely to be far more careful about what you use, waste and lose than may have been the case in urban experience. If your water comes from a well or other source on your own land, it will probably cost you nothing and your only real problem will be to make sure that the supply is pure and remains so – local council Environmental Health Departments will usually check this. If, however, the source is on your neighbour's land – and this applies as much to private leads off his main supplies as to those from natural sources – you need to be very sure indeed that you have all the rights necessary to keep it flowing. In particular, if your predecessor had to pay your neighbour for his water supply, the right to it will depend upon the personal agreements which exist and will not run automatically with the property. These points matter, for it is very expensive to bring a new public water supply in over significant distances.

Remember also that in its natural state water may be alkaline (particularly in chalk and limestone areas) or acid (in moorland and other areas, particularly those where clay predominates). Alkalinity is only a problem in that you may end up with scale deposits which clog your kettles and hot water systems, but unless you wish to replace your plumbing frequently and risk an explosion in any hot water boiler, a water softener may be vital in an area where the mineral content is high. Acidity is far more serious for it corrodes iron, and dissolves and ultimately destroys copper and lead and other soft metals used in plumbing and central heating systems. Acid water also leaches aluminium out of rock and soil and aluminium may reach potentially harmful levels in acidic supplies. Public water authorities are under a duty to keep aluminium in public supplies below levels defined as safe and they usually also correct acidity in mains supplies by adding lime. But if you have a private supply which is acidic you may have to correct it yourself or risk the consequences, and if its aluminium levels are excessive your only option may be to risk it or pay for an alternative. In any event, if the supply to your new house is acid you should have all the plumbing which you intend to retain checked carefully.

Electricity and telephone

If electricity and telephone are not already connected to your country house, the local electricity board and British Telecom will soon tell you whether they can be and at what cost. Bear in mind that the spread of cellular networks may soon make detached cellular telephones cheaper than new fixed connections.

Any electricity supply which comes overland for a significant distance may be subject to interruptions – long or short. Overhead lines are vulnerable to lightning and storms, and in rural areas tractors and other vehicles seem to aim unerringly for their supporting posts. Low powered petrol or diesel standby generators are now fairly cheap and while they will not provide enough power for heating they will keep your refrigerator, freezer, lighting and electronic equipment going. That includes the control equipment for gas or oil central heating, but not the heavy load of electric heating.

If you install a generator, regulations require you to route your mains supply through an approved isolation switch, so that your generator cannot feed power back into the main and risk electrocuting anyone trying to repair the line while it is running. But it may be worth the trouble: a generator can be an important life support system in the country even if years elapse before you need it. In particular, if your central heating is controlled by electricity, you will be very relieved to have your own if a storm or blizzard knocks the public supply out for weeks, though no small generator will supply enough power for electric heating.

Generating your own electricity may even be feasible if your country house has a good river or stream running through it. You can calculate the theoretical power (P) available in a water source with the formula:

$$P = \frac{F \times H}{11.8} \text{ kilowatts}$$

F is the rate of flow in cubic feet per second, and H is the vertical height in feet through which you can design the flow to fall.

Your local river or water authority may well be able to advise and help if you want to harness water power – you will require their approval for any scheme anyway, even if the source is entirely on your own land. You may have to pay them something for the water used, though the tendency so far has been not to charge for purely domestic generation.

You do not face these problems in harnessing wind power but the technical problems and costs of wind power are far greater, and there is not much chance of it being economical unless the wind blows steadily and without wild extremes over your property for most of the time.

Gas

If your rural house is not connected to a mains gas supply or within easy reach of one, you will have to do without gas unless you decide to install a large bulk storage tank and all its ancillary equipment and take regular deliveries as with oil. If you have available substantial quantities of slurry from cows or pigs, you might experiment with producing your own methane by installing the equivalent of a large septic tank (see the section below on Sewers and drains). However, the technical difficulties are enormous and while the principle is widely used in bulk sewage treatment, those who have tried it on a small scale have usually ended up with very little gas from very large applications of time and money.

Sewers and drains

If your rural property is connected to public drains and sewers your urban experience will suffice. If it is not, however, it may already drain to a cess pit or a septic tank, with surface water to a soakaway, or be capable of being so drained. Remember, however, that you need enough land available at the right level to accommodate a cess pit or septic tank and that Building Regulations govern their size, structure and location – particularly if health or water is at risk.

There is an important distinction between cess pits and septic tanks. A cess pit is a sealed tank which receives and contains all the foul drainage from your house. Under Building Regulations its capacity must be at least 18 cubic metres and as soon as it is full it has to be emptied. There are contractors in most rural areas who will do that, but it costs money every time, usually more than the drainage rate it saves you.

A septic tank has a drainage outfall at its top. The principle is that foul sewage drained into it is digested by the anaerobic bacteria naturally present in excreta. The solid matter forms an active crust on the surface and the relatively clean water below flows continuously through the outfall into an adjoining soakaway and the surrounding soil. The capacity of a septic tank must be at least 2.7 cubic metres.

So long as nothing interrupts the natural anaerobic process an adequately sized septic tank may continue to function efficiently, without being pumped out or requiring other attention, for years. But if you put bleach (sodium hypochlorite) or other bactericides down the loo or the drain you may kill the bacteria. Your septic tank will then seize up, fill solid and need pumping out just like any cess pit.

There are alternatives to bleach on the market which are specifically marked safe for septic tanks, particularly for the loo. But if you end up with a septic tank and bleach has played any part in your urban life, make sure that you and all your family understand why it should no longer go down the drain.

Finally, if your cess pit or septic tank is on anyone else's land, or if it may have to be, make sure that you have full and adequate rights to use and get to it.

Space and water heating

Oil, gas and electricity
If you value convenience beyond anything you will heat your rural house with gas, oil or perhaps electricity and it may already be so heated. But the cautions already given in the discussion of stand-by generators should be remembered or you may find yourself without any heat in the worst weather.

Solid fuels
Solid fuel – including wood if available – may guarantee you warmth, not least because you can buy and store it in quantities sufficient for long periods. But apart from convenience solid fuels also raise special problems.

Wood and chain saws
Wet wood only yields a third, and dry wood half, of the heat of the same weight of coal, so do not retain or commit yourself to wood burning unless you are sure that there are ample supplies at reasonable cost in the locality, and in comparing the cost of wood with coal remember that you must buy more wood for the same amount of heat. If you intend to use wood, remember also that it pays to accumulate your stock well in advance of need so that it has plenty of time to dry out.

The salt in sea driftwood quickly corrodes iron and other metal wood burners, so if your rural house is near the sea make sure that driftwood has not been used in any such stove and that you do not use it yourself.

If you have timber – not subject to any tree preservation order – on your own land or available on that of others, acquiring and learning how to operate a petrol driven chain saw *safely* may be essential to its use. The emphasis on safety is deliberate. You can sever limbs, have eyes flicked out by flying splinters, or have your skull cracked by a falling branch through a moment's inattention or bad luck. So a construction worker's hard hat, goggles, leather gauntlets, heavy overalls with no loose ends, steel-toed boots, and ear muffs to protect your hearing, are vital parts of the kit. In addition, you should never plan to use a chain saw from a ladder or without your feet being firmly planted, and if possible you should always have someone else with you but standing back.

Burning wood deposits large quantities of wet and clinkered tar in conventional cold chimneys and the tar soon penetrates walls and discolours any plaster on them. Several different types of flue lining are available to prevent this, though none of them is cheap. Any old flue may also allow flue gases to percolate through the walls – possibly with fatal consequences – so have any in use checked to minimise the risk of gassing yourself. Installing a modern double-walled metal insulated flue may be sensible whatever fuel you plan to burn. It will often be cheaper than building in a new one.

Chimney fires
Chimneys can be a fire risk in old houses, or in any house if they are not regularly swept. Chimney sweeps seem to be a dying breed, but it is not difficult to do the job yourself; rods, hooks and brushes are relatively cheap, and they do double duty if you ever need to rod out your drains.

Once ignited soot and wood tar burn fiercely and any structural combustible material which penetrates the flue, as it may in old houses, is soon aflame. In addition, the updraft erupts large lumps of burning soot out of the chimney and puts anything inflammable in the roof at risk. One precaution, taken particularly by some with thatched and timbered houses, is to run water pipes up the chimney so that water can be turned on and poured down at the first sign of fire. That may work but the mess brought down is horrific; if you adopt that precaution, or if your predecessor has, you need to make sure that no one turns the taps inadvertently.

Solar panels

Over the last two decades solar panels have appeared on an increasing number of houses. At its best the sun does not deliver more than 1.5 kilowatts of heat per square metre in the latitudes of the British Isles and that best is only achieved around noon on clear days near Midsummer Day. An array of solar collectors large enough to recover significant heat in winter is likely to produce a substantial excess in the summer, and no solar collector functions to optimum level unless it can be steered to follow the sun in both elevation and azimuth – like Jodrell Bank's radio telescope. Most domestic solar installations are fixed and relatively small and likely at best to contribute limited energy for parts of the year, most frequently to domestic water heating.

If solar heating is already installed in your country house you should have the system checked carefully. If water or another liquid capable of acting as an electrolyte flows through the solar collectors, you need to know what materials are exposed to the flow and how they are protected against corrosion: if a mixture of metals such as aluminium, copper and solder are involved, naturally occurring electrolytic corrosion can soon punch holes in the system. In addition, water may freeze and you need to know how the system is protected against that.

If the system has an appropriate heat transfer oil flowing through it, with the hot oil then exchanging its heat into water, perhaps through the coils of a standard indirect hot water cylinder, it is likely to be safe both against corrosion and frost. But oil can percolate finely through metals such as copper, and the price of that safety may in time include the finest of oil films on your hot water.

If you plan to install solar heating yourself, check the economics carefully. It may take 20 years or more to recover the usually high cost of proprietary systems – which may not last that long. Designing and installing a system of your own which uses plumbing components generally available may yield far quicker returns.

Heat pumps

The energy yield of heat pumps, which collect heat from air, soil or liquids may be two or three times that needed to drive them. They have been used to advantage by farmers who need both to chill their milk and heat water for the dairy. But it is doubtful if they are yet economic on a domestic scale, and if your rural house does not already have a heat pump, installing one should probably have low priority.

Caravans in the garden

By law anyone may station one caravan within the curtilage of his private dwelling house and use it as an extension of his house. But planning permission and a caravan site licence must be obtained before such a caravan may be used as a separate dwelling (see Chapter 7) and that applies equally whether the occupiers of the house let the caravan or the occupiers of the caravan let the house. If, therefore, your rural house already has a caravan which is separately let, or you plan to have one and that is significant to your plans, make sure your solicitor knows about it before you commit yourself.

Restored houses

If your rural house has been previously renovated or restored by people who have thereafter lived in it for some time, the chances are either that they will have done the job properly, or that any deficiencies will be clear on close inspection. But there are people who make a business of buying old properties, doing them up, and immediately reselling them. Not all these people are obviously in that business and some of them take the easiest and most profitable course by tackling the visible problems and burying the remainder under a new coat of plaster and paint. So if you are interested in a newly restored house, you need to know in detail exactly what has and has not been done and as far as possible what the condition was of everything covered up. Unless you are prepared to take the risk, you also need to have all that defined in writing in terms which will give you a contractual remedy if anything seriously defective has been hidden before you commit yourself. As to that specific guidance from a solicitor may be essential. Remember particularly that no inspection, even by a surveyor, will reveal things which can only be discovered by carving into the fabric of a house, and since no one is likely to allow you to do that against the prospect that you might buy, requiring them to come clean in writing is usually the only practical alternative.

Common land

If there is the slightest risk that any part of your house or land may have been registered as part of a village green or common under the Commons Registration Act 1965, or if it is said that in buying it you will acquire rights over some common, make sure that you ask your solicitor to search the Commons Register specifically. Commons, and the problems to which they may give rise, are discussed in more detail in Chapter 6 and nothing about them is necessarily obvious or rational, so have regard to that chapter in forming any judgement.

People using your land

If someone else has been allowed to use your land – or if you allow him to use it – he may be or have become an agricultural tenant protected by the Agricultural Holdings Acts. That leaves you with hardly any right to stop him. If such a person has been, or is, granted permission in writing to do no more than graze the land for a period which cannot exceed 364 days, that permission or grazing licence will prevent him acquiring the protection of the Acts. That applies also if, after the end of the 364 days, another similar permission is granted, so long as the one before it did not include any right to a further licence. But if the paperwork has not been, and is not, scrupulously maintained – for whatever reason – a protected agricultural tenancy may still result. So if there is any hint of someone having used the land with the country house you want to buy, you need to alert your solicitor to the possibility. And if you want to let someone use it after you buy, come hell or high water, make sure you see a solicitor, have the paperwork right, and keep it that way.

Checklist for your rural house

1. Have you considered the implications of the existing fabric,

equipment and grounds of the house which interests you? (See also detailed checklist in Appendix 2.)

2. If only to leave yourself with a right to compensation if something serious is missed, have you asked a professional surveyor to survey it?

3. Might your use of the house be restricted by planning controls? In particular, is it a listed building, in a conservation area, or are trees round it subject to tree preservation orders? (See also Chapter 7.)

4. Is there anything in the immediate neighbourhood which may be or become a nuisance? (See also Chapter 8.)

5. Is there any possibility of the house being affected by common land or village green status? (See also Chapter 6.)

6. Is there any indication that anyone may have been using any part of the land attached to the house for grazing or other agricultural operations?

Chapter 4

Horticulture and Animals

Space to grow your own produce and keep animals may be one of the things for which you aim in moving to the country. Your objectives may be entirely the pleasure, relaxation and additional quality which can be derived from growing flowers and other things in your garden and keeping pet animals. They may also include profit: the indirect profit which you achieve by producing fruit, herbs, vegetables and animal products for your family which you would otherwise have to buy and which contribute to your family's standard of living; or the direct profit of producing for public sale.

If you intend to make a significant contribution to your income with the sale of produce, you will be subject to exactly the same constraints and economic conditions which govern professional farmers and market gardeners. You will be unwise to attempt to compete without something at least of their know-how, resources of land, equipment and finance.

But you may be legally liable for certain things – damage or injury caused by dogs or livestock which escape, and some regulations which govern disease in or transport of animals are examples – whatever the basis of your undertaking may be. If you sell any hens' eggs – however few – your hens must be regularly and expensively tested against salmonella under the 1989 Testing of Laying Flocks Order.

The chances are that if you intend a commercial operation you will prepare yourself for that, so we will concentrate on the things you may do for leisure or for private family advantage.

Before considering specific things, there are some general observations which may be helpful.

The benefits of growing your own

You will already realise that there may be qualitative advantages in producing some of your own food. You know what you put into it, and so do not have to take on chance the components which may have been included in the chemistry set of the commercial producer. You know that your produce will be fresh and that it has not travelled days, maybe weeks, between its originator and your local shop.

However, it may not have occurred to you that if you can take things straight from the garden to the kitchen, unlike the commercial producer, you can grow varieties of fruit, vegetables and herbs which taste good though they do not travel well, and would lack the regular, polished appearance of goods on a supermarket shelf if they did.

This can make quite a difference. In developing strains for commercial production plant breeders have had to concentrate on varieties which resist apparent decay and preserve a fresh appearance for long enough to remain attractive when they reach the shops. But flavour has often been a casualty; and, regardless of appearance, enzymes of decay start destroying food and food values as soon as any food is dead. Food which is the seed or tuber of its plant – cereal grains, peas, beans, potatoes, carrots, parsnips and swedes are examples – does not usually die immediately it is cropped. But most cut green vegetables and soft fruit – lettuce, cabbage, strawberries and raspberries, for example – do die on being cropped and a corpse is still a corpse however remarkably it preserves its texture and appearance.

The economics of producing for yourself also differ fundamentally from those which govern the commercial producer who must usually concentrate on producing large quantities, with each individual item showing very small profit when sold over the farm gate. Everything you produce for your own family saves you its *retail* cost paid out of your taxed – in some cases means-tested – income. The value item by item is far greater and, though the reward of an individual lettuce may not seem much when paralleled against the reward you can win from time spent in your accustomed occupation, it all adds up. A large garden yielding a wide variety of produce can knock £1000 a year or more out of the expenditure of a family who previously bought everything.

Your time, energy and cost

Of course, it is very difficult to produce anything without time, energy and some expenditure. Will you have the resources? If you can eliminate commuting when you move to the country, that alone may release all the resources you need; but even if you cannot, other members of your family may have the time; and insofar as you produce things for yourselves you will automatically save the time and cost of going to buy them.

Energy is often the greatest concern. It is hard work digging gardens, and very hard if you plan to cultivate the 600 or 700 square metres which you may need to use if you intend to make a significant contribution to your larder. However, it is the cultivation and planting at the start of the season, and the harvesting at the end of it, which create the peak demand both on time and energy; and it is the peak demand which determines the size of the area you can cultivate effectively – and limits, if you are sensible, the scale on which you will try. In between the peaks a bit of weeding and hoeing may be all that is needed; and gardeners who are not too worried about weeds re-seeding themselves know that even that can be dispensed with once plants are strongly established.

You can go a long way towards flattening out the peak demands with a large deep freeze to take surplus yields, a limited amount of garden equipment and – so long as you are prepared to use it – a handful of substances in the modern chemical armoury.

Rotovators

With a rotovator – purchased for convenience or hired from a tool hire centre – you can in a weekend clear, and subsequently cultivate ready for planting each year, all the land you are ever likely to need to use. If you have not previously used a rotovator you will be wise to consider one which is driven by wheels separate from its cultivating rotors, and which preferably has a reverse gear and possibly several forward ones. Sturdy rotovators are heavy, and having to haul them from your shed to your land, back out of tight corners, or operate them at one speed regardless of ground conditions can be as rough on your back as digging.

Greenhouses and general equipment

A greenhouse will also help significantly. In it you can bring plants on early for later planting in open ground (where seeds for peas and beans may be dug up and eaten by mice before you see anything of them); and in it you can later grow things such as tomatoes, cucumbers, green peppers and melons which flourish in the open only in the warmest and most sheltered parts of the country. One of the popular 12 x 8 foot aluminium framed greenhouses is often enough; but unless you are prepared to risk seeing your greenhouse taken to pieces in some gale, anchor it on strong foundations where it is sheltered from the wind (though not, of course, the sun). It is worth considering putting any greenhouse on a platform which has some drainage but is otherwise flagged or concreted. Then you can build up beds of soil within it; water and plant roots will not sink down into, or rise up through, the soil on which it rests; and at the end of each year it is much easier to dig over greenhouse beds which rest on a hard floor and to dig in and retain the benefit of more manure or other fertiliser. You may have to be more careful about disease and insect pests building up within such an enclosed system. But washing down the internal glass each year with water containing bleach (not to be poured into your septic tank afterwards, of course), and using specific garden remedies for any pests which appear will probably keep these firmly under control.

With these two items of equipment and with basic garden hand tools – spade, fork, handfork, hoe and rake – you are likely to have all the essential equipment for growing your own food using minimal amounts of time and energy. A petrol-powered strimmer may additionally be useful, particularly for cutting off weed heads and cutting back rough areas of grass or hedgebank surrounding your cultivated land. But you can manage without.

Chemicals and fertilisers

Unless you are dedicated to wholly organic food production, you will benefit further, in time and yield, by using some chemicals, though you should always read carefully and observe the attached instructions for their use. Slugs and snails, for example, can devastate your crops and a series of wet years with mild winters seems universally to have favoured their increase. There is no natural substitute whose efficiency in controlling them compares with chemical slug bait; and while onions, garlic, shallots and leeks are usually fairly immune you may find that using it is the only way to avoid serious damage to virtually anything else you want to grow.

You may have manure, compost and other organic material available to sustain the texture and fertility of your soil but you will be lucky if you have enough. Everything available should be used; but if you test your soil with one of the soil test kits available from most garden centres (and this should be done in several places for there may be wide variations even in a small garden) you may still find it deficient in one or more of the vital chemicals – nitrogen, phosphorus and potash. In areas with acidic soils you may also find that you need to use lime or slag to reduce acidity and release what fertility there is; and since heavy rain can wash fertility down and out of any soil, and particularly light and pervious soils, it may pay not to break or cultivate your ground until the early spring, notwithstanding all the stories about autumn digging.

If your soil is deficient in any of the vital ingredients, adding small quantities of the chemicals which supply them may be the only way to make sure that your crops are not stunted, your yields low, and the area of land required to give you something worthwhile so large that you cannot comfortably cultivate it.

Weedkillers may also have a place in the scheme of things. Some selective weedkillers are fairly benign and a broad leafed weedkiller which attacks things like nettles, buttercups, docks, plantains and daisies but does not harm grass or its relations can be very useful in removing those weeks from lawns, paths and stray corners from which they may also seed into your cultivated ground. Of all the modern weedkillers those containing glyphosate are probably the most universally effective and radical –

literally, since after being sprayed in very small quantities in solution on green growth it kills most plants right down into their roots. Glyphosate is particularly useful for clearing ground which has long been uncultivated; and, in the garden, for spraying on all weeds after crops have been lifted in the autumn. By spring the ground may then be virtually clean of living weed and that makes cultivation and future weed control a lot easier.

Some of these chemicals are expensive and some inordinately expensive if you buy them in the quantities and under the proprietary names usually available to the gardener in retail shops and garden centres. In most rural areas, however, there are agricultural merchants supplying the same chemicals in far larger quantities to farmers. A single bag of agricultural fertiliser may, for example, cost you little more than a fraction of the same material packaged for the garden and it will last you several years if kept dry and sprinkled in the sparing quantities you are likely to need. Commercial fertiliser is made up for specific crops and the proportions of nitrogen, phosphorus and potash included are balanced to their specific needs. But the bags are always marked (20:20:20, for example, means 20 units each of nitrogen, phosphorus and potash – always in that order) and for general use both in the greenhouse and the garden one bag of an equally balanced fertiliser is likely to meet all your needs.

Agricultural merchants also supply bagged quantities of lime, slag and slug-bait and will advise on and supply appropriate weedkillers. Some of these may still be expensive – a litre of weedkiller containing concentrated glyphosate may cost around £20, for example – but that will still be a lot cheaper, and last a lot longer, than the gardener's equivalent.

Rabbits, pigeons and grey squirrels

If pigeons, rabbits or grey squirrels are common in the area in which you choose to live, they will quickly discover any fruit or vegetables you try to grow and will then devastate your crops. Expensive netting cages are rarely an answer – grey squirrels will soon chew their way through plastic netting and may not take long to do the same with wire. Rabbits will burrow under anything. Shooting these pests is often the only relatively cheap solution – the legalities of firearms are discussed in Chapter 5. However, if you start by shooting regularly, the survivors will soon learn to give your garden a wide berth. A vigorous initial campaign may protect you for a long period after it is concluded.

Grazing animals

You may, with less demand on time and energy, be able to bring more land into a use which is productive for you and your family be keeping animals to graze it, saving you some of the effort of cultivation. They will also complement your gardening by consuming waste vegetable matter and yielding valuable manure. But before considering specific animals do remember that fruit and vegetables give you the best value: the margin between the cost of the seed and what you have to invest in their production and their retail value is much greater than that between the initial cost of livestock, their feed and care, and the retail value of their product. Herbivores and poultry will find some of their food in land over which they range, but you will almost always have to supplement that with cereal and other products probably bought in, particularly because the nutritional value of grazing diminishes from summer to winter.

In addition grass and other grazing land may require lime, fertiliser, and occasional cultivation and re-seeding if it is to give of its best. If the number of your stock is small, and the area of grazing large, your animals may still be able to range over it and find enough to allow them to flourish: this is why so many mountain areas which defy any other economic cultivation are grazed by sheep or deer. But remember that the amount of useful food which any animal can win out of natural grazing depends on the size and number of animals competing for it; and while all animals benefit from space in which to stretch themselves, they need a lot more space over which to find food than they do merely for their welfare. A couple of sheep or goats may find significant quantities of food in half an acre or so of land. A single cow or horse will need more.

Specific animals

We turn now to some specific animals. So far as keeping them gives rise to rights and (mostly) liabilities, bear in mind that the law cuts both ways, benefiting you if you suffer loss as well as burdening you if you cause it. But remember also that the fewer the number of people you have round you, the more you will need their goodwill and friendship: sorting out major difficulties amicably and tolerating minor ones is usually far more important in the country than hammering away for pounds of legal flesh.

Dogs and cats

If you keep a dog your main worry is the legal liability to which that may expose you. The law is the same whether you live in town or country, but the risks you run in the country are greater. You are liable anyway if your dog causes damage or injury as a result of your negligence – a man who unleashed his dog while walking it so that it was free to dash across a road causing an accident provided a specific example. But you have to do, or fail to do, something specific yourself to be guilty of negligence, so that risk is limited. You may also be prosecuted under the 1871 Protection Against Dogs Act, fined, have your dog ordered to be destroyed, and have to pay compensation if you keep a dangerous dog and it causes damage or injury. But the fact that the dog is dangerous has to be previously known – hence the legend that every dog is entitled to one bite.

If you own a dog, however, or are in control of one, you are automatically liable if it harms livestock on agricultural land (except your own land) by attacking or chasing it, or is free in an enclosure containing sheep. The owner of the stock can recover compensation from you and you can be fined up to £400 under the 1953 Dogs (Protection of Livestock) Act and the 1971 Animals Act. In addition, under the latter Act anyone who has control of livestock or owns land with livestock on it can shoot your dog without having to compensate you if there is no other reasonable way to stop it worrying his animals; he can also shoot it if it is still on his land after his animals have been worried unless it is under someone's control or there is a practicable way of finding out who owns it.

The National Farmers Union estimates that dogs kill more

than 10,000 farm animals every year, and seeing an animal which has been attacked by dogs is horrific. Most farmers keep and love dogs themselves, but, hardly surprisingly, more and more of them shoot any dog they find on their land regardless of the fine print. If your dog is shot you may afterwards not be in any position to prove that the rules were not observed; and may also identify yourself as the owner of an otherwise unknown dog and land yourself with financial liabilities if you try.

The country may increase your ability to roam free; but if you are wise it will extinguish your dog's, particularly since even the most placid dog may become a killer if it joins up with others and they hunt as a pack. You will no doubt take all the care you can to prevent your dog causing harm: but if you do not, you will soon earn the hostility of your neighbours whatever the penalties.

No one is likely to be able to guarantee containing any dog all the time; and while most household insurance policies now automatically include cover against claims to which dogs give rise, those claims can run into tens of thousands of pounds if animals are damaged, and hundreds if people are, and it is vital to check that you have insurance which is sufficient.

Cats do not attract the same risks. But again relationships will quickly sour if your cat slaughters your neighbour's young poultry or devastates his aviary, and anyone facing substantial losses might attempt a claim against you under the law of nuisance (see Chapter 8).

Poultry – and their predators

You may decide to keep or rear poultry – hens, ducks, geese, turkeys, guinea fowl, pea fowl or any others – for their eggs or meat, for their attractiveness or for both. There is a lot to be said for not having to travel to buy your own fresh eggs and poultry meat, and for knowing what its sources have eaten. But do not imagine that there is much cash advantage in keeping any type of poultry unless you plan to do it on the large and intensively controlled scale of those with whom you will then be competing – after allowing for cost and feed every hen is reputed to die a debtor.

Notoriously large numbers of poultry can be kept enclosed in very small spaces – anything from batteries, deep litter houses or small runs onwards. If you keep them like that you will have to provide, and usually buy, all their food; take great care to avoid disease; and, with sensitive animals like turkeys and geese, avoid anything which may panic them into a crush causing multiple deaths and injuries. Chickens in particular will peck away at and ultimately kill any of their number which has even a minor injury. The more enclosed poultry are, the more they are likely to savage each other, hence the commercial practice of cutting off the sharpest point of the beak by debeaking. Ducks and similar aquatic fowl fare best if they have some water in which to which to wet their beaks and clean themselves while swimming. A small plastic ornamental garden pond may be enough for a few of them but do not imagine that anything else, animal or vegetable, is also likely to survive in it.

If you allow your poultry to range free, most varieties will still need, and return to, an enclosed shed at night. However, guinea fowl have an annoying taste for roosting in, and uttering piercing cries from, high trees; and they and other fowl may still lay eggs and attempt to hatch them in concealed hollows in undergrowth where they are highly vulnerable to predators.

The fox – now as much an urban pest as a rural one – is the most devastating slaughterer of any poultry in the open, day or night. Its tactics are impeccable: it will case the ground, bide its time, and launch its raid when it is good, safe and ready. It will bite off and eat the heads and drink the gushing blood of as many birds as it can swiftly reach, and only carry off for more systematic consumption those of the carcasses which time, its strength and its own safety allow. You then face what seems to you like widespread, indiscriminate and senseless slaughter.

Dogs run foxes a close second if they get in among your birds. And mink and polecats, which may also weasel their way into your poultry house, come third. Badgers' preferred food is earthworms, and while an occasional old or sick badger may take poultry, badgers do not deserve the reputation of poultry slayers attributed to them by some country people, which is most often founded on the discovery of poultry remains outside badger earths which have been colonised by foxes.

Any poultry in the open are at risk to predators and you have to balance the advantage of allowing them to range free – for the food which they can find, the better quality of their eggs, and the benefit to their health – against the need to keep a constant eye on them and the risk of their summary execution if you don't. And you have to include also in that balance the damage which poultry will do by scratching and pecking at anything you are growing which they fancy and can reach. Hens and ducks have a huge appetite for all varieties of cabbage and for many root crops and you may have to fence your vegetables in if you want to let your poultry out.

Domestically, bantam hens are often the best single bet for open range poultry. Weighing less than a pound, against the couple of pounds of a laying hen and more for those bred for meat, they are individually capable of less damage. Flighted varieties (not silkies) can fly significant distances if they have to scatter to avoid danger, and that and the fact that they otherwise tend to flock together makes them more secure against predators. They lay eggs which are two-thirds the size of ordinary hens' eggs but otherwise indistinguishable from them, and do not rest from laying with anything like the frequency of larger birds. And they find significant amounts of the feed they need in the wild, saving you buying or providing some of the high protein feed which you will still be wise to give to any poultry if you want the best out of them.

As to feed, remember that all poultry are scavengers and that hens and ducks in particular will make good use of waste meat and vegetable scraps which probably went straight from your town kitchen to the refuse collection.

Larger mammals
The larger an animal is, the greater its need for food and skilled care and attention, and the damage which it can cause if it escapes. Under the 1971 Animals Act you are legally liable for damage caused by any livestock of yours which escape, regardless of whether or not you are in any way responsible for their getting out – and livestock include cattle, horses, donkeys, sheep, pigs, goats, poultry and domesticated deer. You may also be prosecuted under the 1980 Highways Act if they escape on to a highway. No ordinary household insurance policy is likely to cover you against these risks, so if you intend to keep any such animal you should make sure either that existing policies are extended or that you take out specific cover.

You will also have to comply with the rules and regulations, most of them concerned with animal health, which govern particular types of animal. If you keep cattle, sheep, goats or pigs, for example, you will have to record every movement of every animal on and off your premises under the Movement of Animals (Records) Order 1960.

If you have no previous experience of keeping larger animals, you should read up as much as you can about the care of any you choose. If the animals of your choice are commonly kept in your neighbourhood the chances are that, if you ask, local farmers will be willing to help you both with advice and practical assistance with animals which they keep; and often, which is particularly important, with buying sound stock when you start. There are likely to be associations or societies, whose numbers include people of great experience, specific to other stock. It is wise to join the appropriate society and learn something from it before you start.

Large animals (and large numbers of smaller animals) yield significant quantities of manure which can be very useful if you plan to raise produce in your garden. But it will soon accumulate if you do not use it, and that also can expose you to prosecution if it creates a risk to public health or if, with or without any fault on your part, slurries find their way into rivers or streams. Fines for river pollution are frequently in hundreds of pounds, sometimes in thousands: in addition, you can be compelled to pay the cost of restocking if fish are killed – and you may have to pay nearly as much for the fry of some fish as you would expect to pay for them fully grown, cooked and served in a restaurant.

Goats are popular among those who want animals which are both amiable and useful. Often remoter houses have no daily milk delivery and a milking goat may both ensure fresh supplies and save the cost of travelling to find them. However, goats are sociable animals and if you only have one the chances are that it will adopt you for company and follow you wherever it can. Goats seek and need shelter at night and, if the shelter is separate from their grazing, will usually follow you dutifully when you lead them between the two in the morning and evening. Unlike sheep which will mow down everything they can reach, goats are choosy feeders, taking a bit here and a bit there, and they are not an animal to select if you want to keep an area of grass well manicured. Sheep, even geese, do far better. Goats are also supreme escapologists, and if not permanently tethered or strongly enclosed will wander free cutting swathes out of your fruit, vegetable, herb and flower beds.

A good milking goat, which is well fed and cared for, may average at least a gallon of milk a day for 300 days in a lactation (ie the period following its giving birth up to the time when the milk dries up) and if not inseminated may go on giving some milk over two years or more – far longer than a cow. But no lactating animal delivers milk at a steady rate. The flow usually starts when, or shortly before, it gives birth, builds up to a peak a few weeks later and then tails slowly away. So one goat kept domestically for its milk will at times give you more milk than you know what to do with, and at others leave you short. If you keep two it is a good idea to have them inseminated in alternate years. Goats can go on breeding annually and milking for 12 or more years but allowing each a year's break helps to maintain their strength and condition. Unlike cows, goats' milk does not usually separate if previously frozen, goats are not susceptible to tuberculosis or brucellosis, and with a little practice hand milking is fairly easy and swift – 10 minutes, say, to strip a goat out – so long as the goat is not one which chooses to leap around all over the place.

If you keep any lactating animal, however, it has to be milked – usually morning and night – or mastitis will develop which may require veterinary treatment and permanently reduce, even extinguish milk production. Cows and goats, though not usually sheep, still need to have their surplus milk taken off even if you leave their offspring feeding from them and that makes it difficult to go away unless you can find substitute milkers.

Goats will usually bear two kids, often three; sheep one lamb, often two; and cows, one calf and occasionally two. They will, however, first have to be inseminated; and since keeping the male of any large species is both impractical and uneconomic for a small number of females, you will need to know where you can find stud males of any species you keep, or the Ministry of Agriculture artificial inseminator for a cow. Large animals may deliver their offspring without assistance; but there will be times when they need help from a veterinary surgeon who inevitably will charge, or some experienced local who may not.

Failing anything else you may be able to sell surplus lambs and calves in your local livestock market, but there may be no market for young goats; and since a herd of goats will increase rapidly otherwise, you have to be prepared to have some of them killed. If you are not squeamish you can eat the meat of any of your animals which have to be killed – goat meat, of which people have least experience, tastes very much like young lamb if the goat is killed at seven or eight months. But no animal's meat improves with age; no female animal's meat improves if it has already borne young; and the males of any animal intended for food should be castrated as soon as possible after birth. The meat of male goats and some pigs becomes unpleasant and tainted if they are not castrated and, apart from possibly becoming dangerous, uncastrated stock will try and get to any female stock nearby once they are fertile. If they succeed, you may be exposed to claims from the owners of that stock which can be substantial. Any animal may be damaged and injured if inseminated too young; and the offspring of wrongly matched males and females may be worthless.

The idea of a house cow has sometimes been popular among people who move to the country, but a reasonable cow will average 1000 gallons of milk for each lactation, and that, with a growth and decline in yield similar to that of goats, is very much more than most families can sensibly hope to use, consume or milk by hand. It is false economy to plan to feed surplus milk into pigs or back into cows – the milk will cost you a good deal more than the alternative feeds which you will still have to buy anyway. And though you can turn surplus milk into cream, cheese, butter and yoghurt fairly easily – so long as you have the equipment (the main items are detailed in Appendix 1) – you will still end up with surpluses of milk, buttermilk or whey. Producing anything you cannot readily use wastes time and money and defeats the economics of any small-scale operation even if those surpluses can be fed back into your cow or a pig.

You need a lot more knowledge and skill to keep cows than you do sheep, goats and pigs, your financial loss is far greater if they die on you, and you cannot sell their milk or products made from them without having a milk quota and complying with all the regulations administered, usually by the Milk Marketing Board.

Without previous experience a cow is obviously not an animal to keep on the domestic scale.

Many people relish the thought that they will be able to keep a horse, pony or donkey if they move to the country. Still more is it the case that previous knowledge and experience matter if you do. If that knowledge and experience are available from others in your locality you may well be able to draw on it as with any animal. But if it is not, start with smaller animals; acquire experience of them before you work up to something as large as a horse; and gain some experience of riding and horse management from one of the stables you are likely to find in a rural area.

Bees

You do not have to live in the country to keep bees. Hives are kept on roofs in central London, and win much honey from its parks. In the country you may have space which allows you to keep them at ground level without the risk that you and your neighbours will be stung regularly. Moreover, because bees aim first for the nearest source of nectar, a hive will measurably increase the yield of everything in your garden which needs to be pollinated before it fruits. Whether you also win honey depends on the quantity and types of tree and plant which flower in your area and on there being warm, but not too dry, weather when they are in flower. The commonest and most prolific plant sources of nectar growing wild in the United Kingdom are gorse, blackthorn (sloe), sycamore and lime, clover, willow-herb and heather. They flower, usually in that sequence, from early spring to early autumn. If your hive is within three miles of any major growth of these your bees can reach it, and if conditions are good they may bring in so much honey that you can remove and extract the honey as it comes in, largely separating each type.

Honeys are very different in colour, texture, and the rate at which they crystallise from liquid to solid. Gorse honey is butterscotch brown and crystallises within a month or so, so you may have to move very fast if you are to extract it and use it. Sycamore is very dark, with a slightly sour resinous smell and flavour, and may remain liquid for 12 months or more. Lime is very pale and fine, also with a long liquid period; clover is fairly well known and remains liquid for about six months and willow-herb is like lime. All these honeys can be extracted from the comb, leaving it largely intact (and saving the bees having to rebuild it) with a hand-turned or motorised centrifugal extractor. But heather honey is gelatinous and can only be extracted from the comb by pressing, crushing – and destroying – it. It will cost you and your bees ten pounds of honey for every pound of beeswax which they have to build to repair or replace damaged comb, so it pays to shave off the minimum when slicing off the cell cappings before extracting, and to do as little damage as possible to the comb before it is replaced on the hive for reuse.

The commonest and most prolific sources of honey in agriculture are fruit blossom in fruit-growing areas, clover, of course, and the oil seed rape whose dazzling fields of yellow flowers may now be seen virtually anywhere. However, oil seed rape is in many ways a disaster for the beekeeper. It yields vast quantities of water clear honey which, within a week or so of the bees collecting it, crystallises into a hard, almost tasteless, white fondant. So unless you extract rape honey almost as soon as your bees bring it in, it will set solid in the comb and clog it, together with any other nectar brought in, into a mass which defies removal. Therefore, if rape is a major nectar source, or the only one, in your rural area, keeping bees for honey may become an expensive and fruitless pastime. In any event in our climate extra pollination may be the only reliable benefit of beekeeping – so much so that many commercial beekeepers now make a living not from honey but by taking huge pantechnicons containing hundreds of hives on contract to the major fruit-growing areas.

Beekeepers as a class are particularly friendly and willing to help and advise newcomers to the craft, so if you are not allergic to bee stings, or are prepared to take scrupulous precautions if you are, you can with confidence hope to gain any necessary experience by joining your local beekeepers' association. Membership of an association may give you access to cheap, even free, equipment and stock; it is also likely to include insurance against the losses you will otherwise face if your bees contract one of several virulent diseases and have to be destroyed, along with a good deal of your equipment, under supervision of Ministry of Agriculture bee inspectors. Council Environmental Health Officers often call on local beekeepers to remove swarms of bees, and may be able to put you in touch with them if you lack any other point of contact.

There are, however, things you should bear in mind from the start in planning to locate a beehive. Bees prefer hives in sunny sheltered positions. They fly out from them, up, and then back again, in and from the direction of the sun. So their flight path follows the sun across the sky during the day. On flat ground they are not likely to tangle with or sting anyone nearer than 20 feet or so to the hive unless they are in a bad temper. But that distance may extend if the land rises above the hive so that at some stage in the day they have to fly downhill towards it. If the weather is thundery, or the season is one in which bees are constantly short of food and often swarming because of starvation, they may range angrily 50 yards or more from the hive and sting anything they can; and if before dusk you replace on the hive a honey super containing comb from which you have extracted the honey, the whole hive may erupt and any living thing within 100 yards or so may be stung on the off-chance that it was responsible for the theft. Fortunately, you can avoid that risk by making sure that you only replace extracted supers late in the evening: by morning the bees will have forgotten, or have their minds on something else.

Unless your family are indifferent to bee stings, put your hives in a place where the bees' characteristics will not bring them over ground which your family has to use regularly – or too close to it. And show the same concern for close neighbours. Keeping bees does not normally give rise to legal liability to others, though it might if their number and location amounted to a nuisance (see Chapter 8); but it may swiftly send relationships with neighbours on a downhill spiral.

General

Growing your own produce and keeping animals is something anyone can learn by reading, trial and error and drawing on the experience of others. But the basic rule with the care of any growing thing which is new to you is to start small. You will learn and produce a lot more far more quickly if you start with a small area of ground and work out from that, even if you have acres of land. Only practice will show you what yields you can expect from what crops in what areas of your land and, if you are not producing commercially, unusable surpluses merely waste your time, energy and resources.

The same applies to animals. People who move to the country are sometimes tempted to buy immediately every type and number of animal they wish to keep. If you have not previously kept an animal, or a particular type of animal, you will have no real idea how much time and what food and other resources it will demand. You will make progress which is far more secure if you start with one type – usually the smallest – in limited numbers and then build on that experience. You can add numbers and varieties as you become sure that the resources remain to look after them and that taking them on meets your family's aspirations. And, after all, if you intend your move to the country to endure, as most do, you should have plenty of scope for evolutionary experiment.

Checklist for your garden produce and keeping animals

1. How well will existing land, building, fences and facilities meet your plans? (See also Appendix 1 for tools and equipment you may need.)
2. Are you insured for all risks which keeping animals may involve?
3. Have you considered your legal duties in keeping specific animals?
4. Do your plans risk nuisance or pollution to your neighbours? (See also Chapter 8.)

Chapter 5

Neighbours, Social Life and Recreation

'Do they accept you?' may be the first question your urban friends ask after you have moved to the country. It reflects an anxiety which seems to be almost unique to those who live in the crowded areas of England; and it is a curious anxiety both because so many of their forebears came from the country, and because it presupposes that country people are somehow entirely different from everyone else, which of course they are not.

The differences of style and expectation which do exist are due more to the differences between the stability and enduring nature of rural life than to any difference in the people. Many rural families have been based in the same area, sometimes the same settlement or house, for generations. The idea of having an extended family, which includes relations, friends and neighbours and which ensures the mutual support upon which life in remote areas sometimes depends, is natural to them. It was once natural to everyone: indeed, the first generations which moved from country to town took it with them. That was the origin of the widely observed communal strength which existed in the first settled old city areas before they became slums – later to be razed and their people and communities scattered; it still survives in undisturbed industrial communities like the valleys of South Wales.

Your modern urban community is the product of the industrial need for mobility. When an individual must move, maybe several times, he cannot take everyone else with him. It is that which has honed the modern urban family down into the smallest – and most enclosed and vulnerable – unit which is capable of being mobile: husband, wife and any children. And as more and more women also have and must choose careers, it is that which is shaving even that unit down still further into solitary individuals and single parents.

The more remote a rural area is, the more natural are the habits and customs of the extended family. They include an efficient bush telegraph, often feared by town people, which is likely to make sure that who you are and what you do is widely known almost before you arrive. It is not there merely or mainly to feed prurient gossip, though few humans are free of an interest in gossip or soap operas and tabloid newspapers would never sell. It is there to make sure that if anyone ever faces significant trouble, that fact is known and neighbours can help. They will not usually intrude on your life at all unless you invite their help or company; but they will know if you really need help and will be there like a shot to offer it. Hardly ever will you hear of someone lying dead or uncared for for weeks in a house in a remote area.

Inevitably, the extent to which this significant difference survives depends on the remoteness of the rural community you choose. If it contains a large majority of urban people, many of them commuting back to a town, and has long been colonised it may not survive at all. Such societies may not differ in any significant way from those to which you are already well accustomed in any suburb.

If it has been rural until recent times, and has then received a substantial influx of urban people, both ways of life may continue in parallel and you may be able to choose between them, The indicators of such a parallel existence may be subtle – two Women's Institutes, one singing Jerusalem and inviting lectures on all sorts of rural and other subjects and another with a disco and a wine and cheese party as the highlights of its annual proceedings, for example. They may hide in no more than people's attitudes: if you ask villagers what the village means to them, one may say: 'Well, I was born here, my father was born across the road, and my grandfather was born in the cottage next door so I suppose that's what it means to me.' Another may merely comment: 'Well it's 10 minutes walk to the main line to London, three miles to the motorway and eight to the airport. Of course, we may not stay here very long but it's a nice place to live.'

If, however, you move to a more remote area containing few migrants, you will find congenial friends and acquaintances among them – the more friendly usually because they have trod the path before you – but your general social life will depend entirely on the extent to which you join and support the rural pattern.

There are odd localised exceptions where historic conditions have driven small communities so tightly into corners of their own that their reaction to any newcomer may seem almost psychotic; but individually the large majority of country people, including people in areas where Gaelic or Welsh may be the natural language, are inordinately hospitable and friendly. The fewer people on the ground, the less each of them is devalued, as anything may be by excess. And through long experience they know, as you may not yet realise, that a time may come when anyone may need the strength of his neighbour and they cherish each relationship accordingly.

There may, however, be significant distinctions between individual and collective responses, as there may be anywhere between those of individuals and the crowds into which they congregate. People in areas where there is a powerful sense of cultural or historic identity – as there is in Cornwall, Scotland, Wales and Ireland and particularly in those places where a natural and native language still prospers – have struggled for centuries to preserve that identity.

There are still those alive today who remember children having to stand in a corner at school with a wooden board tied round their neck because they used the Welsh which was their natural language at home.

However sensitive you are to such collective instincts; however much or well you seek to master any indigenous language; and whatever your own origins, if you move into such a rural area, and particularly if your greater urban wealth allows you to pay more for a house in it than anyone living there might easily find, you may still seem to the collective consciousness no more than a modern extension of historic repression. In such areas, therefore, you may always have to face, and must be prepared to accept, the possibility of an ambivalence between the warmth which is natural to all countrymen as individuals, and something far cooler from their aggregate. And because the second is less conscious and more subtle you may have to be more sensitive to it even than you are with individuals.

If you move from an urban to any rural community, it is desperately easy to throw a spanner in the works without even realising it. Universally, the easiest way is to start by believing that inevitably you know, have seen, or have done more than anyone you are likely to meet there. Without any obvious indicators you may run into someone who himself was at least as significant in an urban community as you were not so long ago. But you would also be wildly wide of the mark if you believed that the majority of people native to rural areas inevitably lack the extent and breadth of your own experience.

Two recent urban immigrants illustrate that mistake. The first insisted to a group of elderly locals, against a quiet but repeated suggestion that it was the local lighthouse, that he had seen the northern lights in July. One of the locals wryly remarked afterwards: 'I was on the trawlers up into the Arctic Circle for 40 years: I know the bloody aurora borealis when I see it.' The second bought a pint of beer for an elderly local farmworker saying 'Well John, I suppose you've never travelled very far from here.' Politely John agreed. But John had left the United Kingdom with the British Expeditionary Force in 1939, had been evacuated from Dunkirk, had served with the Eighth Army right through the North Africa campaign and up into Italy and had then fought with the Chindits in Burma until 1946. When he finally came home he vowed never to go anywhere else again.

If therefore you move to a remote rural area it pays to listen and feel your way very quietly, very carefully, and very sensitively for a long time.

Communal contacts

The more remote a rural area is, the more pubs, churches and chapels will be primary meeting places. If you work as well as live in the area, however, your work will also bring you into contact with people; any children at school there will add to your contact – as it does anywhere. Any contribution which you make to a rural community will increase your acceptance by it, provided you contribute with reasonable humility, and the degree of acceptance generated by each contribution will be substantially greater than you might have expected in an urban area. But bear in mind that people long established in rural areas have networks of relations and friends which have endured for generations; and while they may well welcome you into their family group, that does not make you part of their family any more than welcome into a smaller urban family might do.

Special interest groups, societies and associations flourish more vigorously in rural communities than in urban ones. Discovering those which exist, and joining those which interest you, gives another significant entrée to rural life. Many of these societies have urban counterparts but again there will be differences. Organisations like Rotary International, for example, normally only accept one representative of each type of occupation, though rules sometimes prove elastic. In a town, however, there may be plenty of potential candidates for each category; in a remote area there may only be one. But he will be far more significant in that community than his urban counterpart in his, and more often than not will also be a far more significant human being.

The economics of rural life may also make a difference. The markets promoted by the Women's Institutes nationwide, though not restricted either to women or to WI members, offer scope to earn income in remoter areas which may be far more material, and need to be won in a far more businesslike way, than in markets close to towns. The fare offered in these rural markets is often of superb quality, and their management and quality-control techniques have to match it.

Now, again, some specifics.

Rural schools

Rural schools may be small and widely scattered. More pupils may have to travel longer distances to reach them, though school transport should be available for any younger child who has to travel more than two miles, and any older child more than three. The smaller the number of teachers and pupils in a school, the greater the impact of their quality – or, occasionally, lack of it – but the reputation of rural schools can be discovered by local enquiry as can most rural reputations.

Generally, rural schools offer far more educationally and socially than their urban counterparts despite proportionately more limited resources. The gap between the most and the least able teachers is anyway far narrower than that separating their pupils: the fact that teachers must have sufficient ability to be accepted for training alone ensures that. And since teachers are no less likely than you to prefer rural living, particularly when salaries may be the same wherever they teach, the odds are that rural teaching quality will be high.

Children's characteristics also matter. If there are fewer children each school is likely to have smaller numbers of any given range of ability than an urban counterpart. But the prospect of each child being taught to the limit of his ability increases when numbers are smaller and, particularly, if children come from stable homes in a stable community in which discipline and manners are instinctive. The more remote a rural area, the more that will be the case, and that may also encourage good teachers to stay and to move in. One who did so was asked, shortly after, by a former city colleague: 'What's it like to teach real children again?' That really says it all.

The academic achievements of rural schools may be smaller in number than those of larger urban schools, but that is inevitable if the rolls are smaller. Only between 1 and 2 per cent of the population of the whole country has high flying ability. But if you take the number of children in your rural area, calculate the number who might be expected to have great ability on a national basis, and divide that by the number of schools locally available to them, you are likely to find that each produces at least the quantity of high flying performances you would expect. They may also produce individual high performance in specific subjects – from the purely academic through music, art and drama to more exotic topics – which utterly transcend national experience. The chances of a child with one overpowering ability may be far greater in a small rural school.

The only difficulty you might face with rural education, and then only in remoter areas, comes at the end of secondary education. If your child has no recent experience of urban life, he or she may only have the vaguest conception of some of the options available; and the horizons and goals of the teachers may be more limited than in more heavily populated places. But, if you do feel that, it will only be because of your own previous urban experience: and if you have that experience the chances are that you can do something about the problem yourself.

Rural medical services

All the medical services you expect in urban life are available in rural life. The only difference is that the more sparse the population, the more you may have to travel for any of them – from chemists through general practitioners to local general and specialised hospitals. In remote places the telephone is a vital link between you and medical help, though even CB radio may be better than nothing.

Despite greater distances general practitioners may be no less (or more) willing to visit your home than they are in towns, though their nose for people who need, and conditions which demand, home visits may be sharper for that also follows in communities where people know each other and their circumstances more personally.

The problems of distance will be bridged – for patients – with ambulance, sometimes even helicopter, services. But nothing will shorten the delays to which the need to travel may give rise. As remoteness increases, therefore, you yourself have to be more perceptive of conditions affecting your own and your family's health so that, where possible, you spot and tackle urgently anything which might otherwise develop into a crisis. If you do not already keep a substantial first-aid kit – including a clinical thermometer which may give vital early warning of real trouble – you should make the purchase of one a first priority following your move. And if your existing medical skills and knowledge are vestigial you should improve them quickly. Your local branch of the St John Ambulance brigade may help in that; at the worst so may a medical dictionary. However, do not kid yourself that you can learn any more than what *might* be wrong from a book, or be tempted to pick the most benign option and do nothing. If you have to open your book at all your safest next move is to get to your local doctor as fast as you can.

Distance also creates problems for those who have to visit people in hospital. Your car may solve those. But if it fails, or if you do not have one, the chances are that your neighbours will help you, and rural organisations often come to the aid of those who must visit hospitals regularly.

Social services generally

Like medical services all other social services are also available.

Distance is usually the only problem in calling upon them. Again, there are usually similar alternatives to those which exist in medical need. Bear in mind, however, that nationally both medical and social services are geared to the number of people in the indigenous population and that their establishment generally assumes an average age balance. If you move to a popular retirement or holiday area, therefore, you may find that you have to wait longer for attention because there is an excessive proportion of elderly people in the local population, or of holiday-makers needing emergency treatment in holiday periods.

Rural pursuits

Open country does not automatically imply that you have free access to it, a subject which is treated in detail in Chapter 6. But space inevitably gives you a greater chance to enjoy the countryside and country pursuits and that may be one of the factors which has attracted you to it.

For a start the traditional options – hunting, shooting and fishing – are usually available.

Hunting

Your local hunt will offer another focus for significant social contact whether you joint the smaller number who ride with it, or the larger which attends the meet and follows it. Your chances of joining and riding with the hunt depend on your resources – a horse from somewhere and the ability to stay on it are, of course, fairly essential. They will also depend on how fashionable a hunt is, which usually in turn depends partly on how close it is to a major centre of population. You are not likely to face much difficulty in joining a hunt patronised primarily by local farmers in a remote area. But joining a fashionable hunt where everyone is in full hunting dress may be rather more difficult than joining a select London club and it will almost certainly be more expensive.

Virtually all animals hunted traditionally are now protected against that fate by law – foxes and, with some restriction, deer are the only exception. But if you are sensitive to the interests of the quarry it is worth bearing in mind that, with most land now enclosed and farmed, hunting is an even more ineffective means of catching anything than it probably was in history. Indeed, most members of most hunts risk far more harm to themselves, and occasionally their horses, than they ever do to any fox or stag. It is also worth remembering that man is the only predator capable of controlling the numbers of foxes – or deer where they are hunted; that if their numbers are not controlled they multiply and their competition erodes the numbers of other wildlife down to very low levels; that foxes will then turn to domestic fowl, young lambs and vulnerable sheep, and other food sources (including refuse awaiting collection) to sustain still greater increase; and that deer will turn to arable crops.

Far more foxes and deer are killed by other means than by hunting. Many die or are maimed in road accidents, by shooting, or by roaming dogs. Foxes are snared, sometimes even poisoned. But, however it may be, their numbers have to be kept down by us if they are not themselves to decimate many other things, domestic and wild, which we value in the countryside. That is the context in which the social value and attractions of hunting have to be balanced against the occasional fate of the hunted, and to which you may politely have to accustom yourself even if you do not subscribe to it.

Shooting

Understandably all firearms now come under increasingly strict control which also extends to more powerful air rifles. You may not acquire, possess or own any firearm or its ammunition without first obtaining the appropriate certificate or permit from your local police force, and certificates may well be refused without reason given. All firearms are covered by the provisions of the Firearms Act 1968. Certificates for firearms other than shotguns are only granted – if at all – for specific firearms, for specific quantites of their ammunition and for specific purposes. If you are already a member of a recognised shooting club, you may be granted a certificate for such a firearm for sporting purposes. If you require one for vermin control – foxes and maybe pigeons and so on – you may be granted a licence if you have sufficient land of your own on which it may safely be used, or have previous written consent from other landowners to use it on theirs. Automatic and semi-automatic weapons are not permitted and, if you have previously been licensed to hold a semi-automatic weapon, the police are likely to call it in and adjust it to single shot capability when your licence is next renewed. Calibre 0.22 rifles with telescopic sights are probably the weapons in commonest use for vermin control though larger weapons may be required and permitted for deer hunting. However, since even a 0.22 rifle might kill at up to three miles range, the need for control and for great care if you have one hardly requires emphasis.

The rules, and police attitudes in the country, are marginally more relaxed for shot gun certificates. The lethal range of a shot gun is measured in tens of metres rather than miles, though a shot gun with its scatter of shot may be far more devastating than a rifle at close range. You may, however, be able to acquire a shot gun certificate when any other firearm would be refused.

Even if you are lawfully in possession of a firearm and its ammunition you commit a criminal offence if you use it other than on your own land or on land over which you have previous permission to shoot, and if you trespass on land with a firearm, whether or not you use it. You also commit a criminal offence if you discharge a firearm, or are in possession of one which is loaded, on a public highway, or discharge one near a highway causing possible danger to people on it. You need to remember that public footpaths and bridlepaths are public highways. If you intend to shoot for game – grouse, pheasant, partridge, deer or other animal so classified – you need additionally a game licence and you should not carry a firearm which is uncovered in any public place, or leave one visible in your car.

Subject to the legal constraints you may enjoy shooting – anything from clay pigeons and inanimate targets to permitted animals. But if you do, make sure that you are also well acquainted with the essentials of firearm safety – do not in particular carry a loaded firearm without the safety catch on or climb gates or fences without first unloading. You also need to know the customs and expectations of any with whom you may shoot. You may be invited out with a local shooting party; but if it is spread out, for example, and in the excitement of the moment you fire at some animal passing between or over you and your companions, you may not be asked again whatever the results.

Fishing

You need a fishing licence or permit for virtually all fresh water fishing unless you do it on water within your own boundary, and even for that if you fish for game fish such as salmon, trout or sea trout. British Waterways issue licences or permission for canal fishing, river authorities and riparian (that is river bank) owners for river fishing, and the owners of lakes or ponds for those. If estuarial and sea fishing is available, you will have to comply with legal controls on the nature and size of any nets you may use and the fish you may catch – again salmon and sea trout are particularly controlled – but you may also be subject to local or general restrictions on the fishing of particular types of fish. Established local sea fishermen are your most likely source of information on what is locally permissible.

Other activities

Other rural pursuits inevitably also depend on what is available, though all pursuits are likely to be cheaper than you will have found them in urban surroundings. You will almost always be able to have attractive walks and perhaps rides. If there is open water you may be able to sail or indulge in other forms of boating though, inland, only with the consent and possibly formal licence of its owner. You have no automatic right of access and the probability is that there is also no general or public right along any inland river, though that issue is being contested in the courts.

If a river or estuary is subject to the jurisdiction of a port or harbour authority, you will have to comply with its rules, regulations and by-laws and will be wise to study them in detail. They often also control things like paragliding above the water.

If you go beyond that to the sea you will not need permission to use it though you will have to comply with navigational restrictions and to observe, for example, controls on any area used by the Ministry of Defence. But if you decide to put down a mooring in any tidal water, legally you require the consent and approval of the Crown Estate Commissioners, apart from that of any port or harbour authority. The Commissioners' property includes the foreshore and sea bed below high water mark reached by ordinary tides (see further Chapter 6).

As to cultural life, insofar as there are accessible public theatres, cinemas or concert halls you have them to draw on. Most of us now also have radio, television and recording and reproduction equipment available, though reception may be difficult in remote and mountainous places and you may have to use great ingenuity in setting up aerials and use boosters as well. Rural areas frequented by tourists often also offer periodic music and other festivals – local council tourist offices will supply details of these. In addition many rural schools, alone or in combination, sustain orchestras and other cultural activities which may be of quite exceptional quality, though their performances, while usually public, may not be well advertised. It is well worth contacting your local education authority for information if you are interested.

Checklist for social life

1. Will living in your chosen area require particular sensitivity to the feelings of those native to it and if so are you and your family prepared for that?
2. Do you appreciate and accept the power of the rural grapevine?
3. Have you drawn on local experience of schools and other educational facilities?
4. If you are interested in hunting, shooting or fishing, or may need to have a firearm, do you appreciate the legal constraints?
5. Have you checked out the availability of any pursuits which particularly attract you?

Chapter 6
Enjoyment of the Country

You'll be a fairly rare individual if your plans for moving to the country do not include the thought that you will be able to wander free through fields and lanes, over downs and hills, or along coasts and sea shores, and maybe gather the wild fruit and flowers you find there. So far as taking wild flowers and plants is concerned, however, you must disillusion yourself very quickly. Most of them are now protected under the Wildlife and Countryside Act 1981 and other legislation and it is a criminal offence to take those which are. The same goes for most wild mammals, birds and their eggs.

But you are certainly likely to have greater scope to enjoy the open country, so long as your enjoyment does not include taking or damaging things. And you may be able to gather blackberries, sloes, elderberries and other fruit from hedgerows, and maybe mushrooms and other edible fungi if you can find them. Anything on the verge or hedge of a road frequently used by motor vehicles is likely to be coated with an invisible film of motor fuel combustion deposits, and these will include potentially toxic lead until lead free petrol is in universal use. Although it may appear attractive, any wild food found along busy roads is often best left alone.

In approaching any land which you do not own, you should always remember that someone else always does own it: and that however vast its extent may seem by comparison with your own, the owner knows its extent and often its detail as precisely as you know yours. All animals are acutely aware of the extent of their own territory and may even fight to defend inches of it and humans are certainly no exception. And if the tenant or owner of open land finds some stranger wandering over it, his feelings are not likely to differ significantly from those which you would experience if you found a stranger wandering through your garden.

Whether or not you have any legal right to be there you may be able to roam freely over open land in the country simply because there may be no one around to stop you. But if you have no legal right, it is common courtesy to ask permission of the tenant or owner before you start, and particularly if you would like to use the route regularly. The lawful occupier of land may not have any real legal sanctions if you trespass without causing damage. He can order you off, use reasonable force to remove you if you refuse, and might conceivably obtain an injunction to stop your trespass if it is so persistent as to become a nuisance. But he can only recover nominal compensation against you, unless you cause damage measurable in financial terms; and, if nominal compensation is all he gets, he will probably have to pay his own substantial costs. In those circumstances you are not likely to end up in court.

He will, however, still be your neighbour, and if you ignore common courtesy the news will travel and you will be hallmarked by your bad manners. For the reasons discussed in Chapter 5, sooner or later you are likely to need your neighbours' goodwill, and ordinary courtesy to each of them is part of the price of earning and keeping it.

So also is observing the country code, whether or not you have any legal right to be on other people's land. If gates are closed when you reach them you should always close them after you. You should try to avoid climbing fences or walls, and be careful not to damage them if you have no choice. You should not walk through growing crops, and should remember that grass is also a growing crop. Even if a path runs through a field, or you believe one does, and even if a farmer may have acted illegally by ploughing and sowing it, it is better manners always to walk round the edges and headlands left by the plough. Finally, unless you have specific permission, do not wander all over land, run dogs free on any of it, or allow your children to do so.

One would like to think that everyone knows all these things anyway, and you probably do. But experience makes it all too clear that some who should either do not, or forget at the critical time. Very well-informed people, who in the cold light of day must have known better, have been found romping around, particularly with their children, on farmland. Some have even played games or flown kites or model planes on it. That, incidentally, can be as perilous as carrying long fishing rods or any similar object in any area where electricity is carried by overhead wires: one contact and anyone at the other end may be electrocuted. So if there are overhead electricity cables in your area, the lives of the members of your family may be a good deal longer if you impose an absolute ban on anything which reaches into the sky.

More specific things may seem so obvious as not to need mentioning, except that people still do them. Farmers who have incurred the costs of growing crops are not well pleased if they find someone having a picnic in them, still less if anybody takes new potatoes or other things they are growing. You cannot now be transported for life for stealing turnips, but taking crops is still a criminal offence which may be prosecuted under the 1968 Theft Act. Nor do farmers rejoice if they find tin cans, bottles or other litter left on their land, particularly if some farm animal eats it and then dies or has to be destroyed. And they loathe anyone who lights fires or drops burning cigarettes, pipe tobacco or matches. Fires – deliberately lit or caused by cinders which are not as cold as they look – may race away into standing crops, woodland or undergrowth causing vast damage. Finally, though few country people will ever refuse a request for water, it is not very pleasant if people help themselves to supplies which are probably charged by metered quantities, particularly when many people are far better at turning taps and other piped water sources on than they are at turning them off again.

The question of public rights of way has already surfaced, insofar as they might affect your own land, in the context of rural houses in Chapter 3. We now turn to the detail of these and other rights of access which you have to the land of others in the country – or, more dangerously, may wrongly believe you have.

Public footpaths and other rights of way

Public roads usually define themselves by their finish, furniture and use. As with all rights of way, however, your right, even on a public road, is merely to pass and repass, with or without an appropriate vehicle or animal, and obstructing their surface with a parked vehicle or anything else is technically an offence, except in a defined parking place.

Public footpaths, bridlepaths and similar rights of way may have identifying signs and be enclosed; but they may not be defined at all. The key to their legal existence, and to your right over them, lies in the maps and schedules prepared originally by your local council under the 1949 National Parks and Access to the Countryside Act and maintained since under subsequent legislation. These records also require revision from time to time since existing paths can be closed or diverted, and new ones opened, under statutory procedures in the Highways and Planning Acts.

So the only way to be certain that a public right of way exists is to go to your local council (which will either hold the relevant plans and maps or be able to tell you which authority does), inspect them, and if need be ask for copies. It is worth reiterating that Ordnance Survey and other similar maps cannot be relied upon. They show tracks which exist on the ground. They do not show whether you have any legal right to be on them, and most Ordnance Survey maps carry a note to that effect.

If a public footpath exists you have the right to pass and repass over it on foot only. On a public bridlepath you may additionally take horses. On an unmade public cartway you may additionally take anything you may take on a road, as long as the cartway is wide enough. However, the public right on many cartways has now been, or may be in the course of being, downgraded to that of a bridlepath or footpath.

Your rights extend only over the precise route of the path: you trespass if you wander off it, though no one is likely to be able to do much about that if the path runs over open land and its route is not clearly defined. Even undefined paths are likely to pass sooner or later between some enclosed point or gateway, often ancient. If they do, that point or gateway defines the widest vehicle or object which is capable of using the path, though mainly that limits the use of cartways. If, however, you rely on, or wish to use, such a cartway, do not imagine that you can indulge in some road improvements of your own and widen it for your own vehicles: if you try that the owner of the land over which it runs can, if he is so minded, obtain a court injunction to stop you.

Because public rights of way follow a specific and defined course, they may be interrupted altogether if swept away by natural events. Cliff and riverside paths often suffer this fate when their substance collapses into the sea or is swept away. If that happens the local authority responsible for such a path may create a new route round the gap if the owner of the surrounding land is willing to agree – dedicate is the legal word – a substitute route. It may also create a substitute by making a compulsory footpath order under statutory procedures, though it may be reluctant to do that as those procedures also include compensation for the landowner affected. But new or substitute rights of way can also still come into being simply by people using them regularly, openly and without permission; and unlike private rights of way this implied dedication does not necessarily require evidence of use over a fixed period of 20 years or more.

A landowner can avoid the risk of finding a new public right of way over his land by obstructing it permanently or regularly. For this reason also, therefore, you should avoid arguments with him about the legality of an obstruction unless you are certain that a public right exists – and preferably even then if you value good relations. A landowner may also prevent implied dedication of a route which is nevertheless still left open, by placing on it a notice in the form laid down by the 1980 Highways Act which replaces provisions originally contained in the 1932 Rights of Way Act. Such notices frequently appear on the approaches to railway stations. These points are equally relevant to you if you own land over which members of the public frequently trespass.

The duty to preserve and maintain public rights of way rests with the appropriate local council, which must also be involved in any application to close or divert them. Any problems over public paths are therefore safest first left to them. However, councils with many miles of public path in their area may not have anything like enough cash to protect or care for them; and some, facing financial stringency, have been willing to enter into agreements with private individuals under which they clear and restore public rights of way as agent of the council. If you wish to re-open a path, and are public spirited and willing to devote your labour and resources to that end, your local council may be receptive to an approach. Mostly, however, such private agency works have been inspired by the commercial interest of those who have volunteered – proprietors of riding schools, for example, who wish to use bridlepaths in the course of their business – and some of these have not seen a very good return on their effort. The right to pass and repass along a highway in the course of business does not extend actually to running a business on it; and intensive use of a path for commercial purposes may amount to that and prompt someone else to try and stop it.

Village greens and common land

There are more misconceptions, confusions and downright errors current in people's minds about rights over commons and village greens than there are about virtually any other rural topic – and that goes as much for country folk as for townspeople. First of all, under the 1965 Commons Registration Act all village greens and common land had to be registered. So quite simply, it is now the case that if land was not registered as either a village green or common under the 1965 Act it cannot now have that legal status whatever its status might have been in history.

The appropriate local authorities (county councils in most rural districts) hold the registers prepared under the Act and can supply details and plans of registered land. You can establish whether any specific area of land is registered by making a formal search of the Commons Register, which is much like the general local land charges searches made habitually by solicitors when they act for you in any land purchase. But the local land charge search does not reveal anything on the Commons Register (and vice versa) so if you have the remotest reason for suspecting that any of your land might have been registered, it pays to ask your solicitor to search specifically. A commons registration will radically affect the value of land to which it relates and what can be done with it; solicitors do not habitually search the register; and while you may be able to claim compensation from them if a search would have revealed a registration and they failed to make one, neither compensation nor a lawsuit may solve all the problems you are left with.

What may be the 'remotest' reason? When you have read the

rest of this section you will know that there may not be any logic to that at all.

There are three sections in the Commons Register with parallels for village greens. The lands section records what land is or is claimed to be common or village green land; the rights section records which individuals claim what rights over that land; and the ownership section records who claims to be the owner of the soil of that land. Under the procedures laid down by the 1965 Act virtually anyone was able to register land as being common or village green land and the formalities were minimal. Many mistakes were made, not least because of the confusion in people's minds – which continues – as to what common land is. Many registrations were based on what was shown as unenclosed land on maps years out of date. Some land which should have been registered was not and as a result has now for ever lost its common or village green status. Far more land was wrongly registered. Cases have emerged where land with long established private houses, villages, even whole hillsides of houses standing on it was registered. Land long established and enclosed in exclusive private ownership, and shown as such on deeds, was registered. What may have been the most costly registration to date involved a small area of land bang in the middle of a site intended for development near a town centre. Its unsuspected registration frustrated the whole development.

For a relatively short period which ended in 1971 anyone who objected to any registration in any section of the registers could lodge notice of objection. Many did. But many more did not: indeed because some of the registrations were so apparently ridiculous, it understandably never occurred to those affected even to think that they might be involved. But the 1965 Act took no account of that possibility. If no objection was lodged to an entry in the lands or rights section, the entry became absolute and final without any facility for subsequent correction. Owners of the soil might still argue about ownership, but that ownership remained subject to the land retaining the status of common or village green land, and to the exercise of any registered rights.

If any objection was lodged in time even to the smallest part of a lands or rights registration, it affected the whole of the unit of land registered, and the status of the whole then remained provisional until a Commons Commissioner sat to hear the case and decide whether or not to confirm all or any part of the relevant registration.

Many objections were lodged in time, so many in fact that in some areas of the country provisional registrations still remain and Commons Commissioners are still sitting to consider them 18 years after the registration date closed. And where the possibility of correcting errors was preserved by even one minute timely objection it has been possible to correct many of them during this process. But unless or until there is further legislation there is virtually no way of changing any registration which has become final. Efforts are being made; there is a private members bill before Parliament at the time of writing.

Why all this matters becomes clearer as we turn to the characteristics of village green and common land and the rights which exist over it.

Public parks apart, village greens are the closest you get in English law to land over which members of the general public may wander about and freely disport themselves. Village green land will always be owned by someone, and be under the protection of the local community or similar council if no other owner is known. But that ownership is of limited value because of the general public right over the land, and because the land may not legally be fenced or used for purposes inconsistent with that right without the consent of the appropriate Secretary of State – which is rarely given. Individuals, may, however, also have specific rights over village green land – to graze animals, cut turf, take clay or other mineral substances (subject perhaps to planning permission – see Chapter 7), even fish if it includes a pond and such rights attach to their property. But no such right now exists unless it was duly registered before 1971 under the 1965 Act, or is guaranteed if the registration is still provisional and subject to enquiry.

If there is an established village green in your country area, you and your family may well be able to disport yourselves on it along with others in the locality. But if your house is alongside it, you need to make sure that your garden is not part of it; and if you are told you will have specific rights over it, you need to make sure they are registered.

Common land shares many of the characteristics of village green land with one important exception: apart from some urban commons to which general public rights of access were created by the 1922 Law of Property Act, and a handful of rural commons over which similar rights have been specifically created, there is no general public right of access to common land at all. If public footpaths cross common land you do, of course, have the right to use those paths as you do any, but that's it.

If that surprises you, as it does many, your surprise is almost certainly because of the word 'common' itself and the use which you know is made of urban commons. So some explanation of why things are as they are may help.

Essentially, common land has always been land owned by one person over which others have specific and defined rights which attach to their property. It may owe its origins to the feudal manors of Norman England. In the feudal manor specific villagers had, in addition to the land which they cultivated individually, the right to graze, and sometimes take part of the natural produce of, the wasteland owned by the manor. That right was common to everyone with similar rights. The commons and the rights attached to them survived. Common land may, however, have quite modern origins: large landed estates were often sold off in lots to those who previously farmed their lots as estate tenants. If the estate included open hill, mountain or other rough grazing, it was not unusual for all the surrounding tenants to be allowed to turn their animals out on to such grazing land under their tenancy agreements; and if they then bought the farms they had tenanted, the sale often included the same rights of grazing open land as were previously exercised under their tenancy agreements. If that happened the open land remained in the ownership of the estate, subject to grazing rights separately attached to a number of properties, and became legally common land. Commons are known which were created in that fashion as late as 1914.

Whatever its origins, land is not common land now unless it is registered under the 1965 Act; no one has any rights over it except those registered and defined under the 1965 Act; the rights of the owner of the soil are subject to any registered rights; and if rights are registered neither the land nor any part of it may be fenced, cultivated, drained or used for any purpose other than grazing and registered purposes, without the consent of the appropriate Secretary of State. Anyone who owns the soil of any such common land therefore owns land of very limited value. If that might turn out to be you, again you need to be careful – as you do if you are led to believe that rights over any neighbouring common attach to your rural house.

The sea shore

Sea shores and the shores of tidal waters inland also have owners. Above the line reached by ordinary high tides, the shore forms part of the land. It is usually owned by those whose more recognisable land adjoins it, unless they or their predecessors have sold it into separate ownership. Below the high tide line, the shore forms part of the sea bed and is owned by the Crown. It forms part of the Crown estate administered by the Crown Estate Commissioners under the 1961 Crown Estate Act.

The Commissioners keep a low profile and neither their role nor their function is widely known to the public. They may enter into agreements with local authorities allowing the latter to regulate use of the foreshore, making by-laws governing its use and so on. They are not themselves in any way likely to pop up suddenly and tell you to clear off the beach because you and your family are trespassing – as technically you are. So, fortunately, although some beaches have been closed altogether in war-time, all of us can usually assume the right to sit, picnic, play or even light driftwood fires on the beach, and bathe from it. Moreover, since adjoining landowners would face impossible problems in restricting use of that part of the beach which lies above the high water mark, we usually have that available too.

Ownership is only likely to intrude when you want to reach the shore or if, being able to reach it, you want something more substantial than recreation out of it or the sea bed. You can only reach the shore as a matter of right along a public highway or right of way which leads right down to it. Take any other route and the owner of the land across which it runs may stop you as a trespasser or charge you for the privilege of being allowed through. If you want to sell ice cream or indulge in any other business activity on the foreshore, its appropriate owner may again prevent you or charge you for doing it. The same applies if you wish to construct or place anything permanent on the shore, or in the sea bed.

The Crown Estate Commissioners may do absolutely nothing themselves to develop their vast underwater and littoral estates, but if any individual or authority comes along wishing to invest in a fixed mooring, pier, fish farming enterprise, or anything else of that nature they will rapidly spring to life and impose very strict conditions which often include substantial annual or lump sum payments. They may even do the same in respect of, for instance, the airspace occupied by a bridge built inland over tidal water by someone who owns both banks. In fairness the Commissioners have offered modest terms to people starting up businesses like fish farming, but even those are subject to future review, often related to the future profitability of the business once established.

So far as planning control is concerned (see Chapter 7) the jurisdiction of planning authorities is a jurisdiction over land, and does not therefore extend to the sea bed below the ordinary high water mark. However, the control of the Crown Estate Commissioners is likely to be at least as exacting; and if you are interested in development of part of the sea bed which lies within an area controlled by a port or harbour authority, you will have to comply with its requirements as well.

Your interest may, like that of the majority of us, lie only in the amenity of the sea shore, coupled perhaps with dabbling in pools, trawling or digging for cockles, mussels, shrimps or prawns, or line fishing. These you are likely to be able to do without any restriction, though you should bear in mind that any sewage in the water is likely to form part of the substance of filter feeders like cockles and mussels, and the diet of winkles, whelks, shrimps and prawns. Nor is it theft to take any sea creature unless someone is rearing it in some sea farming operation, or has already captured it. That qualification should incidentally be remembered and respected if you go skin diving round fishermen's lobster or store pots.

But articles washed up on the shore or on the sea close to it may fascinate you, as they do most of us, and, if you take those, this is different. Here we encounter the exotic field of wreck, which for practical legal purposes includes flotsam, jetsam, lagan and derelict.

A vessel or cargo abandoned at sea by those in charge of it without hope of recovery or returning to it is 'derelict'; things left floating on the sea after a shipwreck are 'flotsam'; things thrown overboard to lighten or save a ship are 'jetsam'; and jetsam thrown overboard with a buoy or marker attached is 'lagan'. All, however, are treated as wreck if they come in shore and are cast up on it.

The legal control of any ship or aircraft which is wrecked, and its contents, passes immediately to the Receiver of Wrecks under the 1894 Merchant Shipping Act and subsequent legislation. Its original owner may reclaim that property within 12 months, otherwise it passes to the Crown. So if you find any wreck or any part of one, you must hand over whatever you have found to the Receiver, following which you may then qualify for compensation for salvage. If you keep it yourself you commit a criminal offence and, apart from the penalty for that, you forfeit any right to salvage, and are liable to pay twice the value of what you have appropriated to the person entitled to it. So if you find, and cannot resist picking up, anything which is or may be valuable on the shore, the only safe rule is to discover who the local Receiver of Wrecks is (usually the local police, coastguard or customs and excise officers can tell you) and take it to him.

Things found and metal detectors

If you find anything of value – in the country as in the town – you have to assume, as you do with wreck, that someone owns it and has not deliberately abandoned it. If you keep it and it has not been abandoned, you commit a criminal offence and may be prosecuted. You can avoid that risk either by reporting your find to the police, and keeping the article found safe at least until it can be established whether anyone claims it, or by handing it over to the police who should then return it to you if it is not later claimed. Only to that extent may it be that 'finders keepers'.

If your find is under the ground – as an increasing number of things have been particularly since metal detectors came into use – the person legally occupying the ground will be its legal owner unless it contains a significant quantity of gold or silver and is subsequently held at a Coroners Inquest to have been deliberately concealed, rather than casually lost. In that event it will be treasure trove and the property of the Crown, though you may receive some compensation for finding it.

If you have a metal detector, remember that the 1979 Ancient Monuments and Architectural Areas Act made it a criminal offence punishable by fine up to £200 to use one in places protected under the Act – usually areas of archaeological importance or scheduled monuments. So it does not pay to improve the odds of finding something interesting by prospecting in such a place; or indeed anywhere else, your own land apart, unless you have previously agreed terms with its occupier, including terms which define who shall have anything which you find.

Fruit gathered

The 1968 Theft Act says specifically that if you gather mushrooms, other fungi, flowers, fruit or foliage growing wild on someone else's land you are not guilty of the criminal offence of theft unless you do it for reward, onward sale or other commercial purpose. Until someone gathers them these things are regarded as being wild things not owned by anyone, but this obviously ceases to be so if you raid someone else's basket. If you gather any protected species you may still be guilty of other criminal offences defined by the legislation which protects them, and that legislation covers most attractive wild flowers and their plants, though not the fungi, blackberries, elderberries and sloes which are perhaps your most likely quarry in the country.

Unless you enter other people's land with permission to pick these things, you are still a trespasser. That applies even if you enter by, and remain on, a public right of way, for your right to pass and repass does not include the right to stop and crop as you go. The legal risk of such trespass may be no more than that which follows any trespass on open land which does not cause damage. But again it is good manners, and conducive to future good relations, to ask first. If your neighbouring farmer likes his mushrooms himself (curiously some do not), he will be even less pleased to wake up and find you picking them than he will be if he merely runs into you as you are walking across his land.

Checklist for your enjoyment of the countryside

1. Remember that taking anything from land which you do not own may involve legal problems; and that, while the law of trespass may be your only concern with wild fruit and fungi, you may become a criminal if you take things of value from the sea shore; wild plants, flowers, animals or birds' eggs from anywhere; any farm crop; and any article found. Using a metal detector may also be a criminal offence on a protected site.
2. Beware of flying kites or model aeroplanes or taking fishing rods anywhere near overhead electric cables.
3. Always observe the country code.
4. Before exercising what you may believe to be a right over any footpath, bridlepath, village green or land reputed to be common land make sure that the right actually exists and that you are entitled to exercise it.
5. Remember that the Crown Estate Commissioners have legal control of all land which lies below the high water mark reached by ordinary tides and that this includes the banks and estuaries of tidal rivers as well as the sea shore.

Chapter 7

Planning Control

Planning control and nuisance

Planning control and the law of nuisance which is discussed in the next chapter are related in a number of ways. One purpose of planning control is to prevent development which may amount to a nuisance – and that goes beyond legal nuisance which, as you will find in the next chapter, is not necessarily what you may think to be a nuisance. In addition, some of the provisions of the Planning Acts deal with specific nuisances and create procedures for stopping them.

On the other hand, the fact that planning permission has been granted for development, or that such permission is not required, does not mean that a use or other development which is or gives rise to a *legal* nuisance is then protected. If someone builds something in compliance with planning control which obstructs your rights of light, for example, you are still perfectly free to take court proceedings to protect your right. If someone creates a legal nuisance by operating premises in accordance with planning control, the same applies. As with all law it cuts both ways: you cannot rely on a planning consent, or any law which spares you obtaining it, to shield you from your neighbours if you cause nuisance to them.

Planning control

Taxation is the activity of central and local government which intrudes most persistently on our lives. In the country planning control may run it a close second. The 1971 Town and Country Planning Act is the cornerstone of present law and if you find references to 'the Act' in this chapter that will be the one intended. Bear in mind that the Act is not all of it. Planning law has evolved over years and now extends into great detail – the standard work used by planners and lawyers fills more than 8000 pages contained in four volumes. At its most optimistic this chapter can only highlight some of the salient points.

Planning control restricts your right, and that of your neighbours, to carry out development of your respective properties. Development is defined as the carrying out of building, engineering, mining or other operations, in, on, over or under land, or the making of any material change in the use of land. If there are trees protected by a tree preservation order on your land, you will need permission to do anything to them. Much of the development which is possible has already taken place in urban areas. Indeed, the consequences probably figure prominently in your decision to get out into the country where that is not so. But once you arrive in the country you may wish to make changes to your house, and you may have to make changes to it or to other property in order to produce a living. Again, your neighbours may be in the same position.

The need for change is more general in the country. There are more old houses requiring improvement, and lower rural incomes constantly encourage those who have them to try and do something about it. This is why planning control becomes more important.

Control may have a bearing on the house you want to buy. It will intrude inevitably if you plan to build a new house; convert a building which is not already a house or within the planning use you wish to make of it; or restore something which once was a house but has been unoccupied so long that its use as such has been abandoned under planning law so that planning permission is required before it may again be so used.

Planning permission may or may not be required if you wish to carry out alterations and some changes of use. Since it costs you money to apply for planning permission, both in fees to the planning authority and in the preparation of plans and documents; and since the planning authority can impose restrictive conditions on you if you do apply, even if planning consent is not necessary, it is important to know when planning permission may not be necessary, and how you can find out if it is. These things therefore figure substantially in the following pages.

Houses you may not be allowed to live in

It is general planning policy to refuse planning permission for any new house or new housing use in the open country. But there are exceptions and the commonest is the house permitted on an agricultural holding of sufficient extent to justify it economically. Such houses are usually restricted to people employed (or last employed if retired) in agriculture and their families, and houses built subject to such conditions remain subject to them. So there is little point in falling in love with such a house, unless you satisfy the conditions yourself; and if you buy, or seek to build, a house subject to such conditions you must remember that its resale value will inevitably be substantially less than that of a house available for general occupation.

Houses subject to other occupational restrictions may also have been permitted under Section 52 (of the Act) agreements. In addition, the government is now considering legislation which will effectively create a two-tier rural housing market in which restricted properties, inevitably cheaper, will only be available to indigenous inhabitants. This is to try and meet the resentment felt by people in rural areas who find themselves priced out of their local housing market altogether when it becomes dominated by townspeople with far greater resources. This resentment is widely felt throughout the countryside and has reached explosive proportions in areas where immigration also intrudes on indigenous cultures. You indeed may unwittingly contribute to it if the price you pay for your apparently low-cost rural house is still far more than any local could pay.

In some areas conditions have also been attached to properties sold out of council housing stock, or those which have benefited from improvement grants, which restricts their future occupation at least for a defined period.

That said, however, it is nothing like as common in the country as it is in towns to find properties whose use of occupation is also restricted by covenants or other terms included in their title deeds, though that also can still happen.

Most planning and title restrictions will show up with the local searches and other enquiries habitually made by any solicitor who acts for you in any property purchase. But local searches do not always correctly reveal the established use of property unless planning consent has been granted for it since consent was first required in 1947; nor may they reveal whether a planning authority will subsequently take the view that an established use has then been abandoned. So although your rural property may once have had the use you wish to make of it or may have recently resumed that use, it pays to alert your solicitor and make specific enquiry if you learn that any property you are interested in has been out of an original use for a significant period.

Enforcement of planning control

Changes of use apart, planning authorities cannot take enforcement action to require the cessation, removal or reinstatement of any development once four years have elapsed from the time when it was carried out. And so far as changes of use are concerned, enforcement action cannot be taken if a property has been used as a single dwelling house in breach of a planning condition for more than four years, or in respect of any change of use which occurred before 1964. But enforcement action can be taken in respect of any other change of use since 1964 for which planning permission was required, however long the intervening period may be since the change was made.

Planning authorities take enforcement action by issuing and serving enforcement notices. They may or may not be accompanied by stop notices calling an immediate halt to the development to which they relate. If you are served with an enforcement notice, you have a right of appeal to the appropriate Secretary of State within the time specified in it – usually 28 days – and the notice will set out the bases on which you may appeal. *But the time limit on your right of appeal is absolutely critical.* If you fail to appeal, the notice becomes final and absolute as soon as the time for appeal expires and the notice then takes legal effect whether or not there was any justification for it. So if you are ever served with a planning enforcement notice and are not content to comply with it, it is essential that you lodge an appeal in time, and take legal advice immediately if you do not have an intimate knowledge of planning law yourself.

Making planning applications and cautions about doing it

You may be able to make a planning application yourself. Planning authorities will supply the necessary forms and it is not too difficult to follow them. It is often sensible to discuss your proposals with the planning authority's officers before you apply: they may be willing to give informal guidance about your proposals, and are likely to tell you if you have no hope at all of succeeding. Overriding general policy often defines zones where specific things will and will not be permitted and that policy is likely to be upheld on any appeal. The boundaries of established settlements within which new housing may be allowed are, for example, likely to be clearly identified, as are those within which specific types of commercial development will be permitted. You can appeal against refusal of planning consent, or against conditions contained in one, usually within six months of the decision. But you must remember the caution already given (see page 107) about applying for a consent which is not legally required; and you should bear in mind that although certain developments may not require permission, some planning authorities may still encourage you to apply. If in any doubt, first ask them for a ruling under the Act as to whether permission is necessary.

Beware particularly if you are already doing something, and some planning officer, who may appear both amiable and helpful, turns up and tells you that you should apply for permission to do it. That may be so. But cases are known where that has happened; where an unnecessary planning application has then been made and refused; and where the planning authority has then issued an enforcement notice to stop the development in hand, often based on the fact that development for which planning permission has been refused is continuing. You can still appeal against such an enforcement notice, but your appeal will be additionally embarrassed by the fact that your own application implies that you yourself thought you needed consent, and the authority's refusal shows all too clearly that you do not have it.

In such circumstances in particular, independent professional advice may be important before you make any move. In cases of doubt, which many are, you may be better off risking the issue of an enforcement notice, and relying on its appeal procedure, than in first muddying the water with a planning application.

When do you *not* need planning permission

When may you not require planning consent? The main circumstances are defined by two statutory instruments made under the Act – the Town and Country Planning (Use Classes) Order 1987 which, of course, relates to changes of use and the Town and Country Planning (General Development) Order 1988 which relates to other development. These orders define various developments permitted in a large number of different types of case in great detail; and we shall come to those aspects of them which may most generally affect you and your neighbours in the country shortly.

Certain changes of use

Before that there are a couple of points which flow from the basic law. As you will recall from the start of this chapter, planning permission is required for a *material* change of use. Not all changes of use are material and there is a very grey interpretative area surrounding the boundary between those which are and are not. Using a room in your home as an office for your business – professional or commercial – or for any sort of homeworking may not, for example, amount to the material change of use which a more substantial business use would. Repairing the odd car in your private garage may not require a commercial garage consent. Installing a microwave oven in your retail grocery, newsagents or other shop so that you can sell reheated pies to your customers, may not turn your premises into premises selling hot food for which special consent is needed. Admitting the general public to watch you carrying out your art, craft or profession, or some interesting farming or other operation, and charging them for the privilege, may not change the use of your premises so long as public admission does not reach a level where its entertainment becomes a very significant part of what you are doing, and your business a side show. Accepting a few paying guests into your house in the summer may not turn it into an hotel or guesthouse for which consent is required. And if you run a business like a farm or smallholding selling your produce is inevitably part of that business and the uses which it encompasses, so you may not need planning consent to establish a farm shop to sell your goods or limited quantities of other people's.

But if your activity generates large flows of traffic to your

111

premises, and particularly if that causes trouble on the roads, the planning authority may try to stop it and may succeed. As an example, an enterprising diary farmer who enhanced his profits substantially by using his milk to manufacture his own ice cream was stopped from selling part of it direct to the public from a farm shop and his appeal was refused.

The grey area of material change of use, and the wide range of uses which may in fact be implicit in some established or permitted uses, may allow you and your neighbours in the country a good deal of scope for doing things without first obtaining planning permission. It is as well to be alert to the possibility. But if your activity has a commercial value and if its goodwill attaches to your property, you may not be able to persuade anyone else later to pay for that goodwill if you sell unless you have planning consent. Many country people who started with a handful of bed and breakfast guests and then slowly developed a substantial guesthouse business without attracting the attention of the planning authority (often also, and hazardously, without complying with the safety requirements of the fire authority) have ultimately run into that problem.

Now we turn to development permitted by the Use Classes and General Development Orders; first the former.

Changes under the Use Classes Order

The principle of the Use Classes Order is fairly simple. Its schedules list a large number of specific general uses. Class A1 covers shops, Class A2 financial and professional services, and Class A3 food and drink. Class B – B1 to B8 – covers a variety of business and special industrial uses. Class C – C1 to C3 – covers hotels and hostels, residential institutions, and dwelling houses; and Class D – D1 and D2 – deals with non-residential institutions and assembly and leisure premises.

Each of the specific class headings in the Order is followed by a list of other activities which fall within the same class; and a property which has planning permission or an established existing use for an activity in that class may be used for any of them without planning permission. So a shop in Class A1 may be used for the display or retail sale of goods other than hot food; as a post office, ticket or travel agency; for the hiring out of domestic or personal goods or the reception of goods for washing, cleaning or repair; and for the direction of funerals. Hotels and hostels in Class C1 may also be used as boarding or guesthouses (and vice versa) as long as no significant element of care is provided for their occupants. And dwelling houses in Class C3 may be used by not more than six people living together as a single household, apart from single people or any number of people living together as a family.

If any of these things are done in your rural property, or you want to do them yourself, or perhaps you are troubled by your neighbours doing them, it pays to have a good close look at the fine print.

Development under the General Development Order

The General Development Order relates mainly to development other than change of use, though some changes of use are also included. It works on a basis similar to that of the Use Classes Order. Schedule 2 of the Order is divided into 27 parts, each dealing with a particular type of development, and many of the parts further set out specific sub-classes of Development – A, B, C and so on – permitted within that type. The permitted development is often defined in great detail, and subject to numerous conditions so again you need to study the fine print very carefully if any issue arises under the Order. The detail is nightmarish but the only way of giving you some idea of what may be possible is to set it out.

Fourteen of the 27 parts of Schedule 2 relate exclusively to the activities of public, utility and other similar bodies and are not likely to concern you in your move to the country, unless perhaps you wish to challenge what they are up to, and we will therefore concentrate on some of the remaining classes.

Part 1 of Schedule 2 (which deals with permitted development in the curtilage of a dwelling house and contains Classes A to H) and Part 2 (which deals with minor operations involving gates, fences and walls (Class A), construction of means of access to unclassified roads (Class B), and the painting of the exterior of premises (Class C)) are likely to be the most relevant to you domestically.

Part 3 adds to some of the changes of use of commercial premises permitted by the use Classes Order; Part 4 governs temporary buildings and changes of use required in construction work; Part 5 relates to caravan sites; Part 6 to agricultural buildings and operations; Part 7 to forestry; and Part 8 to industrial and warehouse development. Later parts deal with mining, mineral extraction and so on.

As to commercial activities Part 5 (caravan sites) does no more than confirm that planning consent is not required for caravans permitted by the Caravan Sites and Control of Development Act 1960. Since caravans and all that may go with them may be of concern to you in your move to the country, the impact of that legislation will be summarised later in this chapter though some of its effects have already been considered in Chapters 2 and 3.

So far as Parts 6 and 7 are concerned a general point only is appropriate here: agriculture and forestry enjoy very considerable scope for erecting buildings and carrying out their operations without planning consent, though that scope is subject to many conditions. If, therefore, you contemplate such development in the country, or again are concerned by the development of others, you should look at the detailed provisions – though you may still need professional advice on them.

That said we return to the parts which apply to houses.

Alterations to the size of your house
Though you may still have to apply for Building Regulation Approval, Class A of Part 1 may allow you to enlarge, improve or alter your house without planning permission. But you can only do that if your alterations comply with all the following conditions:

(a) The cubic content of the resulting building must not exceed that of the original by a maximum of 115 cubic metres or, if less than that, (i) 50 cubic metres or 10 per cent of the original volume in the case of a terraced house; (ii) 70 cubic metres or 15 per cent of the original volume in the case of any other house.

(b) The resulting building must not be higher than the highest part of the original house.

(c) No part of it must come closer to any highway on its boundary than the part of the original nearest to that highway, or 20 metres, which ever is nearest to the highway.

(d) No part of the original which will be increased in height must be increased to more than four metres within two metres of the boundary of its grounds.

(e) The alteration must not result in more than 50 per cent of the ground within the boundaries surrounding the original house being covered by buildings. Other existing buildings must be included in this calculation but not the original house.

(f) The property must not be a listed building,

(g) The alterations do not relate to any part of the roof of the property or a satellite antenna – these are dealt with separately and subject to different rules under Classes B, C and H of Part 1.

There are yet further rules if the property lies in an area which has been specially designated under Article 1(5) of the Order – a national park, for example. In such areas you require planning permission before you can clad any part of the exterior of a building with stone, artificial stone, timber, plastic or tiles. There is no automatic planning consent under the Order.

There are also rules which may result in separate buildings within the boundary of your house being treated as an extension of it and therefore involved in the calculations. Where an existing building will end up within five metres of your altered house, the volume of that building is treated as part of that added by the alterations – and obviously cuts back on their content; and if you erect a new separate building within your grounds which contains more than 10 cubic metres that building will be treated as an enlargement of the house if it is within five metres of any part of it, or in any event if your house is in a specially designated area – Article 1(5) again.

These qualifications may take some of the shine off the provisions of Class E in Part 1 of the Second Schedule. Class E, again subject to numerous conditions which will not be detailed here, otherwise allows you scope to put up all sorts of buildings for purposes incidental to the enjoyment of your house and that may, for, example include a garage, swimming pool and accommodation for poultry, bees, pet animals, birds or other livestock.

Alterations to your roof
Under Class B, so long again as your house is not in an area

specially designated by Article 1(5), you can enlarge your house by adding to or altering its roof provided:

(a) You do not exceed the highest part of the existing roof.
(b) No part of the house fronting a highway then extends beyond the plane of the roof facing that highway – for example, no dormer windows on the front.
(c) You do not increase a terraced house by more than 40, or any other house by 50, cubic metres.
(d) In addition, you do not increase the cubic content of the house beyond the tolerances allowed for general Class A alterations – sub-paragraph (a) at the beginning of this discussion of the General Development Order, page 114.

Under Class C you can make other alterations to your roof provided they do not involve a material alteration to the shape of your house – roof lights and things like that fall in this category.

Porches
You can build porches outside any external door of your house under Class D, and porches can conserve much energy and warmth by creating an air lock which stops cold and wet weather from whistling straight into your house when you go in or out. But if the ground area covered by your porch will exceed three square metres, or any part of it will be higher than three metres off the ground, or within two metres of your boundary fronting a highway, you cannot build it under the Order and must first obtain planning permission.

Hard standing in your garden, oil tanks and satellite antennae
Class F allows you to build hard surfaces within your property – hard standing for your car, for example; Class G to install an oil storage tank, subject to conditions governing its size and location; and Class H, as already mentioned, to install and alter a satellite antenna, again subject to specific conditions governing size and location.

Calculations under the Order
In any case where the rules require a comparison between the original building and the building which will result after your

alterations, previous alterations count as part of your alterations. So if you or your predecessors have already altered the original building, these alterations may have swallowed up part of your scope to do more without planning permission.

Fences, gates and walls
A word now on the minor operations permitted by Part 2. Putting up gates, fences or walls may well be something you want to do. Doing it can sometimes be a source of trouble between neighbours. Provided your building is not a listed building, however, Class A of Part 2 spares you the need for planning permission, as long as no gate, wall or fence erected or altered is higher than one metre on a boundary fronting a highway, or two metres on any other boundary.

New road access
You may also need to construct a new access on to the public highway. If you need that access because of other development permitted by the Use Classes Order, Class B of Part 2 allows you to form it without planning permission as long as the highway concerned is not a trunk or classified road. In rural areas many are not, but you may still be wise to check the position first with the highway authority in case there is nevertheless some restriction within its jurisdiction.

Painting your house
You may be surprised to find that painting your house or buildings – defined as including any application of colour and so also covering limewash etc – enters into the rules at all. However, Class C allows you to paint your house as you will, as long as the painting is not for the purposes of advertisement, announcement or direction. But again, if your house is a listed building any change in its outward appearance may still be specifically restricted.

Caravans
Now, as promised, a look at caravans.

The right to station caravans on land for human occupation – whether residential or for holiday or amenity purposes – has been strictly controlled since the enactment of the 1960 Caravan Sites and Control Act, and it was fairly rigorously controlled under general planning legislation before that. In general, land may not be used as a caravan site – permanent or for touring caravans – unless planning permission has been granted for that use, and a site licence has been issued under the 1960 Act. General planning policy leans heavily against the granting of any new planning consent for caravans, and against permitting any increase in the number of caravans on existing sites, so the more attractive an area is to caravanners, the less likely it is that any application will be granted for a new site or enlargement of an existing one.

If you are thinking of making all or part of your living by running a caravan site in the country, you may only be able to do that if you buy an existing site with full planning permission and a site licence, and you may not be able to increase in any way the scale of the existing business. Some new sites may be permitted to meet special needs or in areas where demand is low, but if demand is low no great profit is likely to follow any consent you obtain.

Most of the exceptions to the control created by the 1960 Act relate to one or a small number of caravans and most of them offer little commercial advantage, though they may have a bearing on your personal convenience.

The exceptions are these:

1. You may locate a caravan within the curtilage – effectively the garden – of your private dwelling house provided its use is incidental to your enjoyment of your house. You may therefore use it as additional living space but it must not be occupied as a separate dwelling. Caravans are often useful in providing extra space for aged parents or other family members, but if you plan that you should make sure anyone in the caravan also uses the facilities of your house with you. As an extension of this, temporary planning permission will usually be granted if you want to station a caravan in the grounds of your house while you carry out building works on it.
2. Your land may be used for no more than two nights by a person travelling with a caravan, as long as no one else is using another caravan for human habitation on your land at the

time, and you have not had any such caravan stationed on it for more than 28 days in the 12 months before it arrives.

3. If you have more than five acres of open land you can allow not more than three caravans to use it – and charge if you wish – as long as you have not had such caravans stationed on it for more than 28 days in the 12 months before they arrive. The Secretary of State may, however, impose further restrictions on specific areas of land.

4. Certain organisations – the Caravan Touring Club, for example – may obtain certificates exempting them from the provisions of the 1960 Act. You can permit those organisations to station caravans on your land for recreational purposes under their supervision and charge them.

5. If an exempted organisation issues you with a certificate, you may permit up to five caravans of its members to use your land recreationally while that certificate is in force, and charge them, though again the Secretary of State may specifically further restrict that.

6. You may also permit your land to be used by the members of exempted organisations, and charge, for meetings arranged by them which do not last more than five days – caravan rallies are an example.

7. You may provide or permit caravans on your land to be used as seasonal occupation for your agricultural or forestry workers.

The remaining caravan exceptions cover building and engineering sites, travelling showmen, local authorities and local authority sites made available to gypsies. They are likely to concern you only if you fall within one of those categories, which is improbable, or are troubled by them. In the latter case, however, you need to bear in mind that planning consent and site licences may not be required.

Conclusions about planning control

You will understand from the detail which has been given that finding your way through to the exceptions in planning law is a bit like picking your way through a minefield – sown with mines which include both finely detailed qualifications and sometimes complex judgements as to how specific circumstances match them. Maybe it was not intended to be easy.

You may well need professional help in deciding whether any particular proposal requires permission, though such help is likely to save you both cost and delay if the end result is that it does not. But again, bear in mind that the Act – Section 53 – gives you the specific right to ask your planning authority for a decision whether any particular proposed development requires consent; that that decision also can be taken to appeal if necessary; and that if you can proceed without permission you will probably end up less restricted than if you apply for a consent which is not required. If the financial risk in going ahead without consent is small, you may chance your arm anyway, but if your plans attract a substantial price tag you do have to be sure.

Checklist for planning control

1. Has the right to use a house or other property which interests you been lost because it has been so long out of its original use that the use is regarded as having been abandoned? If so, do you need planning permission before you can hope to return it to that use?
2. Is a rural house subject to a planning restriction which limits the class of person able to occupy it?
3. Are you aware of the need for immediate and urgent appeal if you are served with a planning enforcement notice?
4. Have you considered the various exemptions from planning control and the desirability of avoiding planning applications which are unnecessary?
5. If caravans enter into your plans or are already located on land which interests you, have you made sure that the special rules governing caravans can be satisfied or are satisfied?
6. Remember that making any change to a listed building or property in a conservation area may require planning permission and that changes may be severely restricted.

Chapter 8

The Law of Nuisance

All legal nuisances are likely to be nuisances at common law in respect of which you can, if you wish, take proceedings in the civil courts for damages and often an injunction to prevent or contain them. A legal nuisance which is a public nuisance (ie affecting a public right) may require action by the Attorney General, which is rare, but private individuals have successfully taken action to stop public nuisances – one case involved a coach firm which parked its coaches on the public highway and effectively ran its business from it.

Some common law nuisances are also statutory nuisances and the subject of specific legislation. Apart from civil remedies, statutory nuisances may warrant criminal prosecution, perhaps by you, perhaps by one or more public authorities. Noise nuisance is the commonest of these.

We will therefore look first at the nature of nuisance generally, then at common law nuisance and after that at the remedies which may be available, additionally or alternatively, for statutory nuisances.

The nature of legal nuisance

Legal nuisance may arise when something passes from your neighbour's land to yours (or vice versa) causing damage, injury or serious discomfort. Some examples have already been given but are repeated in the following paragraphs.

Miscellaneous nuisances

Nuisance includes the roots of your neighbour's trees if they grow under your ground undermining the foundations of your buildings or disrupting sewers or other underground services on your land – but not usually if they merely grow there. It includes rocks or soil which fall off your neighbour's land on to yours; the filaments of dry rot if they spread from his house to yours; it may include smells, vibrations, noise, vermin, smoke, fumes and agricultural sprays and chemicals. Nuisance may include vegetation or its seeds – farmers are required by law to stop the spread of pest weeds like thistle and ragwort by at least cutting them before they seed; and all planning authorities have the power under Section 65 of the 1971 Town and Country Planning Act to serve notice on the owner or occupier of any land in their area whose condition – which may include general dereliction or specific causes like weeds or vermin – adversely affects the amenity of their area. Planning authorities can require remedial action on such land, though many seem reluctant to use their powers.

Nuisances affecting rights of water, way or light

If your neighbour pollutes a water course and the pollution travels downstream into your water, that may be a nuisance – a recent example emerged in litigation involving a man downstream of a trout farm whose organic wastes entered and polluted the river. If he blocks or obstructs your legal rights of way, water or light, that is a nuisance and interruption of a supply through a known underground channel may be, but not of a supply which depends on natural percolation through the subsoil.

Livestock nuisances

Damage caused by trespassing livestock (however they escape) is a legal nuisance, though you are protected against that anyway by the 1971 Animals Act, but it may be very difficult to prove the loss suffered as a result of cattle trespass. If your garden plants, shrubs or greenhouse are wrecked, you can usually price the cost of their replacement from your local supplier. But if livestock get into your growing crops, you may be stuck with all the imprecisions and arguments of experienced agricultural valuers estimating what area has been damaged and what crops have been lost. Comprehensive, clear and immediate photographs of all damage caused by livestock are an essential part of your evidence in any livestock trespass case.

If you suffer extensive crop damage, you may not get anywhere near the true figure of your loss unless you record the precise yield from your damaged fields, the same for the same crop grown in the same season in adjoining undamaged fields, and then calculate the loss mathematically from the difference per acre or hectare. To be able to do that, however, you have to record the tonnages or quantities recovered from each field involved in the comparison. And you may then have to do that in following seasons so that you can show there is no natural divergence. Even with all the science available you may still face a long, worrying, time-consuming and costly argument with insurers who most probably will represent the livestock's owner. Frequently even an inadequate offer in settlement is preferable.

Human trespass

Damage caused by human trespass may be or become a legal nuisance – a farmer whose land was regularly invaded and crops damaged by caravanners from a neighbouring caravan site successfully took legal proceedings against the owner of the caravan site for allowing that nuisance.

Running water and radio waves

If water escapes on to your land from some pipe or man-made channel, culvert, reservoir or other man-made device or obstruction on your neighbour's land, that may be a legal nuisance – though not if it floods from a natural watercourse and for natural reasons. Electromagnetic radiation may be a nuisance: something as simple as a CB set or unsuppressed motor which wrecks your television reception, for example, though those problems are best tackled under the legislation which governs radio transmissions and through the Post Office authorities who police it.

Dangerous substances and things

If your neighbour keeps or accumulates something on his land which is inherently dangerous if it escapes, he will be liable to you for any consequences if it does escape. A leaking reservoir set the scene for that legal evolution and it gave rise to the legal principle of absolute liability for those who keep inherently dangerous things on their land. Anyone who keeps non-domestic animals with naturally dangerous propensities also falls in this category, but so also does anyone who keeps a domestic animal with a known dangerous propensity – a savage bull, for example.

The concept of nuisance is very flexible and the law is therefore able to adapt to and accommodate new nuisances resulting from technological and other changes.

Variables which affect nuisance generally and noise nuisance in particular

There are limits. Damage is an essential of nuisance so if you cannot prove that you have suffered any more than nominal damage – though damage may include injury to your comfort and peace of mind – there may be no nuisance.

Nuisance is also judged by the standards of the average man – if you only suffer because you are hypersensitive, or because you wish to carry out some particularly sensitive process or procedure on your land, the cause of your suffering may not amount to legal nuisance. In addition, it is the standards of the average man in your locality which matter. Long ago a judge observed that what may be a nuisance in Berkeley Square may not be a nuisance in Bermondsey. If your urban neighbour deposits a mountain of manure in his back garden and the stench wafts constantly into your house, that may be a nuisance; but if your rural neighbour has a midden in his fields nearby it may not, for that is one of the things which may have to happen in rural life. Again, if your urban neighbour sets up a crow scarer which explodes regularly with the sound of a shot gun in his garden, that may be a nuisance. But if your farming neighbours use them in the country you will certainly have to put up with the situation during the day-time; and although they should switch them off at night, you may have to put up with them then if they forget or cannot be bothered.

Some things may be legal nuisances merely if they happen – the rocks falling on your land or the dry rot filaments spreading into your house are examples. But others only amount to legal nuisance if their intensity, frequency, duration, timing or repetition make them so and that is particularly the case with things which cause you personal discomfort in your property but do not cause physical damage.

Noise is the commonest of these. The law expects all of us to put up with the ordinary wear and tear of the neighbourhood in which we live. Bell ringing may be or become an infernal nuisance, but you can expect it if you live near a church and will have to put up with it unless it goes on for hours and hours repeatedly. That also applies to churches which have resorted to modern technology by recording their peal and broadcasting it through amplifiers, though not perhaps if the equipment is ancient and the verger forgets to replace a scratchy needle or, as one did, puts one in upside down. You may not want to wake up when your neighbour's cockerels crow to greet the dawn – and they are off very early in the summer. But in the country you are likely to have to live with it. The same may go for the noise of your neighbour's grain dryer or other agricultural machinery which may be silent for long periods in the year but may have to operate round the clock when its season arrives.

As far as the law is concerned, action for things which only become a nuisance because of their intensity, repetition and so on depends on being able to prove all the detail. If, therefore, you fall victim of such a nuisance, it is sensible to keep a diary over several months recording the date, time, duration and nature of every incident. Noise can be measured in decibels and since noise is also one of the statutory nuisances, prosecutions for noise nuisance are often based on decibel readings taken by local council Environmental Health Officers. But timing and repetition may make noise a legal nuisance and the fact that a noise does not register significantly in decibels does not necessarily mean that it is not a common law nuisance. Some permitted maximum noise levels are defined by law: those for particular types of road vehicle, for example, are tabulated in the Motor Vehicles Construction and Use Regulations. So if you have a road running past your rural house, someone may well be able to argue that noises which do not exceed the decibel levels permitted for road vehicles are part of your natural environment and cannot be a nuisance. Noises within those levels from those vehicles will not be; but others may be if timing, frequency and repetition also enter into it.

Nuisances which are not legal nuisances
Some things which may seem like an infernal nuisance may not

be legal nuisances at all. For example, while you may have rights
of light through defined windows, or to your greenhouse, you
have no general legal right to your view. If you buy a rural house
with splendid open views and someone else then obtains
planning permission to put a housing estate behind you, there is
nothing you can do about it – a circumstance wryly reflected in
the joke that every beautiful view in Wales has a row of council
houses in front of it, though fortunately that is not true.

Nuisances which attract compensation though not legal nuisances

Public developments are usually authorised under legislation
which specifically excludes your right to take proceedings in
respect of any nuisance to which they give rise. That legislation
may, however, provide specifically for compensation and with
some developments you have a general right. If public works are
carried out near you – new roads, motorways, or a new or
extended airport, for example, – and their noise adversely affects
the value of your property, you may be able to claim compensation, the cost of sound insulation, or both from the authority
responsible for the development under the 1973 Land Compensation Act as extended by subsequent legislation. And although
that legislation does not apply to the Crown – Defence Ministry
airfields, for example – the Crown, acting usually through the
Property Services Agency of the Department of the Environment, may well treat a claim for compensation as if the 1973 Act
applied.

The importance of toleration

The tolerance which may be expected of you in the country, and
which you will have to show if you wish to maintain good
relations with your neighbours, often goes beyond the boundaries defined by law. Any nuisance anywhere is best resolved by
friendly discussion with its author if that is possible. The law is
always best reserved for those who prove absolutely bloody-
minded, or cause substantial financial loss and only law will
produce adequate compensation. If you are very unlucky and run
into one of those fortunately rare individuals who, like a small
Hitler, takes an inch, then a yard and then a mile, the law may be
your only answer. In remoter country, however, unless they are

locally known as such you may even have to tolerate the bloody-minded, or risk a large and often expanding gap among the limited number of people available to be counted as friends.

Common law nuisance and remedies

Any legal nuisance is likely to be a common law nuisance. Subject to means-test, legal aid is available to cover civil court cases on nuisance, and legal proceedings may be taken in your local county court or, in more serious cases, the High Court. In court proceedings you can claim compensation by way of damages for the financial loss caused by a nuisance and that loss may include an estimate of the financial value of your comfort and peace of mind. More often than not you will also be advised to seek an injunction to prevent the continuation or repetition of a nuisance or, with things like noise, to restrict the times at which a noise may be created. In addition, if you are faced with the prospect of a nuisance arising – someone has started erecting a building which will seriously interfere with your rights of light, for example – you may be able to apply for an anticipatory injunction to stop it happening.

So far as injunctions are concerned, however, you should remember that they are discretionary remedies, and in particular that if you delay taking proceedings, your delay may result in an injunction being refused. So if you sit back and watch your neighbour put his building up, you may still qualify for compensation if it interrupts your rights of light, but you may not be granted an injunction requiring him to remove the building or stop completing it.

Legal nuisances which affect public rights – highway rights, for example – are public nuisances which ordinarily can only be taken to court by or with the authority of the Attorney General. But as has previously been observed, the Attorney General may sometimes step back and let individuals get on with it.

Statutory nuisances and remedies

Hazards to public health including noise, smoke and chemical fumes may also be statutory nuisances whose authors can be prosecuted for criminal offences. Most often such nuisances are investigated by local council Environmental Health Officers, successors to the old public health officers and their Public Health Act jurisdiction. They are the most frequent prosecutors. You may also prosecute a noise nuisance yourself under the 1974 Prevention of Pollution Act, but you should remember that in a criminal case you have to be able to prove the offence beyond reasonable doubt, not on balance of probability as in a civil case. That is why noise prosecutions tend to rest on the hard evidence of a decibel meter, rather than evidence of circumstances. However, circumstances are still relevant and may upset what looks like a cast-iron case based on decibels. On the whole, if your local Environmental Health Officer is not prepared to prosecute, you may be wise to think carefully before doing it yourself, particularly since any fine or other penalty goes to the State, and you may not be awarded an order for your costs.

Some statutory nuisances arise under the legislation grouped with the 1974 Health and Safety at Work Act and may be prosecuted by the Health and Safety Executive and its inspectors – these include in particular industrial chemical fumes and other nuisances originally controlled under the Factories and Alkali Acts. Some may be specific to particular public authorities. Port and harbour authorities, for example, prosecute the authors of oil pollution within the area of their authority under the 1971 Prevention of Oil Pollution Act; and river authorities prosecute those who cause pollution of rivers or streams in their area, whether they cause it directly or because harmful substances have flowed over or through intervening land or ditches. Even if you pollute a stream on your own land, which runs all the way into the sea without ever leaving it, that stream is within the jurisdiction of your local water authority and, apart from its other controls on it, you may be prosecuted if you pollute it.

In the country farm slurry, silage effluent, sheep dip, diesel or central heating oil, waste garage oil and petrol, all of which may devastate natural river life, figure frequently in these prosecutions, and the fact that pollution occurred without any fault on the part of an individual prosecuted is no defence. Regrettably, pollution from sewage works and water treatment process plants owned or controlled by water authorities is not uncommon, and, though this may change if privatisation splits policing from operational water activities, they are not usually very enthusiastic about prosecuting themselves. In some cases, however, private individuals have stepped in and successfully done the job for them.

Checklist for nuisance

1. Is there anything in the neighbourhood of your house which may be or may become a nuisance? Will it be one in respect of which you might take legal action? Will it be wise to contemplate that even if it is?
2. Is there anything in your house or grounds, or anything you would like to do there, which might expose you to nuisance claims by your neighbours?
3. Are there any rivers, streams, ditches, water supplies, septic tanks or cess or silage pits, middens, rights of way, rights of light, areas of higher ground, or animal enclosures on or close to your land, or do any properties adjoin yours, so that you are particularly vulnerable if anything escapes into or from them or if rights are interrupted?
4. Have you taken into account the fact that things natural to your location – church bells, agricultural grain driers or other equipment, noise or smells from farm animals, for example – may be a nuisance but not one in respect of which you can take legal action?

Chapter 9
The Whole Picture: Further Information

Country life can be marvellous if you choose wisely. It is certainly not the nightmare which the huge number of watch-its, dos and don'ts in this book might suggest. Virtually all the cautions which appear in these pages flow from mistakes made by someone at some time in the country. Indeed, quite a few of them live in memory because I made them myself. But very few individuals and families have chalked up really impressive scores of error, some things have only happened once, and the whole reflects the aggregate experience of hundreds of people, maybe even thousands.

But forewarned is always forearmed, and foreknowledge is essential in exercising choice wisely. And while we accept other people's factual knowledge for what it is, our nature is always to resist their experience and to insist on working it out for ourselves. We all know that from the occasions when we try to guide our children. You are not likely to be any different if you make the single strategic decision to move to the country and you too will in the end work it out for yourself – and you will have to.

While this book contains imperatives, or may seem to, and while they flow from real things which have happened to hundreds of real people over years of migration to the country, they are there not to demand your observance but in the hope that, by being stated at all, they will at least trigger a warning light if you confront similar circumstances, and may as a result smooth your path.

Even in contemplating a move to the country you have already a vast body of useful experience, tempered by your urban life, though its extent and precision is unlikely to be a matter of conscious realisation except at times when you draw on it – consider assembling out of it a guide for country people moving to a town, for example! And much of your urban experience will continue to be valid and to serve you handsomely in the country, however remote your chosen place may be. But country living is different – indeed, you would not choose it or have chosen it if that were not so. In country life things of little apparent significance, or taken for granted in a town, may have an entirely different order of importance. And with some things in the country, your best course may be to do the opposite of that towards which urban instinct would guide you.

With luck these pages will have prepared you for some of them.

Only occasionally does this text go into the nitty-gritty of doing specific things. Detail on the host of things you can do in the country – for yourself and your family; for a living; or for a combination of the two – exists already in hundreds of books and other publications and media output. Any bookseller is likely to be able to offer you lists of books on gardening and cooking; on keeping horses, cattle, sheep, goats, bees, poultry and other livestock; on making cheese, yoghurt, butter and wine; on building, plumbing, electric wiring, glazing, carpentry, slating and tiling; on keeping an hotel or guesthouse or running other businesses or any business; on virtually every art and craft known.

If you want a far more legal book on the law of the countryside, for example, you have, among several choices, Tim Bonyhady's paperback *The Law of the Countryside* published by Professional Books. If you want detailed guidance on a huge number of things which you might do on a smallholding you have John Seymour's *Complete Book of Self-Sufficiency* published by Faber & Faber.

There are periodicals with specific guidance on aspects of rural life – *Horse and Hound*, *Smallholder* and *Home Farm*, for example – which can be ordered through your newsagent or obtained by postal subscription. There is the legendary daily performance of *The Archers* on BBC Radio 4, with swathes of rural data wrought into its scripts along with a lot about rural expectations and attitudes. *The Archers* often also discuss rural attitudes to urban migrants, though there is not much said about their aspirations. There is Jeanine McMullen's periodical series *Small Country Living*, also on BBC Radio 4, which highlights a wide range of rural activities and some of the problems to which they give rise.

Any of these can help with the specifics of country living and so may many of the things in this book. But I hope that this text will also illuminate some of the bumps which may lie unsuspected, or whose significance is less than obvious, along the road to getting there; and that it may also help to make sure that, when you do arrive, your big move is as lastingly happy and rewarding as you wish it to be and as it has proved to be, never mind trial and error, for thousands who have gone before you.

Good luck.

Checklist of Useful Tools and Equipment

Note: Items marked with an asterisk (*) usually have electric-driven alternatives which are often cheaper but which will rarely stand up to extended, heavy or sustained use over long periods.

Generally useful in conjunction with many of the items listed under the specific headings below

Work bench and vice; extending ladders and stepladders; sectional scaffolding; large pneumatic-tyred wheelbarrow

Claw hammer; assorted spanners, Stilson and adjustable spanners; pliers; pincers; screwdrivers; pick axe; sledgehammer; shovel; gas blow lamp; solder and flux; plumb line; spirit level; 25-foot extending steel measuring tape; hacksaw; metal files; hatchet; power drill and assorted wood, masonry and metal drill bits

Gardening

Petrol powered rotovator;* petrol powered strimmer;* greenhouse; extra freezer space; soil test kit

Spade; fork; rake; handfork; hoe; shears; pruning shears; water hose; hand spray; watering can; agricultural yard brush

Building and maintenance

Masonry
Petrol powered cement mixer;* cement trowel; pointing trowel; pointing hammer; lump hammer; cold steel bolster and chisel

Plumbing
Copper tube cutter; pipe bending springs

Glazing
Glass cutter; putty knife

Carpentry
Chisels; mallet; hand or electric power plane; handsaw; circular electric power saw; electric sander; brace and wood bits, particularly large sizes

Electrical
Standby generator

Power positive (illuminating) screwdriver; electric soldering iron

Slating and tiling
Tile cutter; lead hammer

Plastering
Steel and wood plaster float; hand-held mortar board

Drains and chimneys
Extending (screw in) drainage/chimney sweeping rods; screw in hook and brushes

Painting and decorating
Paint and limewash/Snowcem brushes; paint roller; wire brush

Livestock

Poultry
Poultry house; suspendable feed hoppers; gravity water feeders; poultry wire

Goats and lactating stock
Animal shed or building; milking machine; cream separator; extra refrigerator space; churn (for butter); press (for hard cheeses)

Stainless steel milking bowls; low milking stool; stainless steel milk cans; hay racks; fence posts; fence post mallet; woven pig or sheep wire; barbed wire; wire stretcher

Beekeeping
Hives; spare hives; spare hive parts and materials; smoker; stainless steel or well-galvanised hand-driven honey extractor (powered for many hives); electric de-capping knife; fine metal/plastic sieves; metal settling tank or capacious plastic vessel; stock of honey jars; bee veil, gauntlets and overalls

Wood burning

Petrol powered chain saw;* large circular log saw if you are lucky; hand cross saw; log splitting axe; felling axe; construction worker's hard hat; goggles; leather gauntlets; steel toed boots; ear muffs; heavy overalls

Houses – Checklist of Things to Look Out For

Note: It is advisable to take a powerful torch with you when you look round houses.

External

Overall
General condition; indications of previous additions or altera-tions, particularly recent alterations; caravans in the garden; any sign of use of the land by an agricultural tenant; possible sources of nuisance nearby; any suggestion of a village green or common land nearby

Walls
Cracks, bulges, hollows or departures from the vertical

Open joints; solid or cavity walls; moss, algae or water marks on surface; lack of any sign of damp course; obstructed air bricks; structures against walls; soil or rubbish above any damp course or above internal ground-floor level; materials used

Roofs and chimneys
Lumps or hollows in roof surfaces; roof ridges undulating or out of horizontal; slates, tiles or ridge tiles slipped, with open gaps, or missing; lead flashings on chimneys or not; chimneys which are crooked, twisted, open jointed, lacking pots or with weeds growing out of them; hollows, bubbles, open joints or cracks in felted flat roofs; ragged thatch; cracked, slipped or rotted rafter ends or fascia or barge boards; gutters or downspouts missing or with weeds growing in them; materials used

External woodwork
Bare or unpainted surfaces; cracks or twists; frayed surfaces or
ragged ends suggesting wet rot; mosaic/jigsaw puzzle like cracks
in surfaces suggesting dry rot; any fungi growing out; algae on
surfaces or woodworm holes; putty missing from glazing frames;
double glazing or not; security locks or not

Access and boundaries
No public highway access; unfenced or open boundaries and
particularly gaps in them; precise nature, type and location of
fences, walls, ditches, hedges, embankments and gates; width of
gates; rivers or streams on boundary; any wall or building built
on a boundary – access over neighbour's land for maintenance or
repair?

Sewers and drains
Cracks, bulges or lack of alignment in brick or other surfaces in
manholes; pipes into cess pits or septic tanks blocked or
obstructed or waste levels low in them; cess pits or septic tanks
near streams, water courses, wells or water supplies; blocked
drains or drainage grids

Manholes at pipe junctions; vehicular access to or (if new
required) adequate land and levels for cess pits or septic tanks

Water supplies
Mains or private, or none; if private, location of source – spring,
well, stream, reservoir, mains supply of adjoining owner; acid or
alkali; legal rights if source outside your land; positions and
numbers of stop taps; supply metered or rated; public or private
source

Electricity supplies
Mains supply by overhead cables or underground or none;
nature and apparent condition of visible cables; single phase or
three phase supply; adequate loading available from mains;
nature of mains earthing arrangements – to supply, earth pole or
by earth trip; location of main meter and fuse box and switch-
board; any apparently old or jungled cabling and switchgear in it;

any sign of overheated cables or fittings; any generator isolator switch if generator used or intended

Telephone
Cables overhead or underground or none; overhead cables passing through trees or other obstructions; visible wear and tear on any external cables; obvious DIY connections

Gas
Mains or stored supply; location of main taps and meter

Radio, television and VHF
Location of aerials and their stability; direction of nearest transmission mast and hills between

Internal

Walls
Signs of discoloration or damp; serious cracks in plaster, particularly if plaster levels differ on either side; plaster rings hollow when tapped; internal walls solid and load bearing or hollow and partition

Roof spaces
Adequate access to the roof space; pipes or water tanks exposed to frost above insulation; visible rot, decay or woodworm in timbers; signs of water on chimney breast or other wall faces; electric cables exposed to rodents; light visible through slates or tiles from interior; upper ceilings insulated and under-slate or tile surfaces felted; ceilings plastered on to lath (old) or plasterboard (modern); ceilings of hard or insulation board; will the size and location of roof and upper ceiling timbers allow any alteration you intend?

Ceilings
Any serious cracks, bulges or signs of damp

Floors and internal timber
Are ground floors solid or timber? If solid, are they laid on

concrete containing a damp-proof membrane or are the tiles or other surface damp proof? Are tiles or flags laid on the earth? If timber (ie boards, not parquet laid on a solid base), do any boards, ground or upper, show any signs of cracks, woodworm, rot or having been cut out and relaid? If the last why? Do any floors move significantly when you jump on them? If they do, it may signify rotted or decayed joists or joist ends or merely that the joists are too widely spaced to give stability (common in old houses, particularly in upper floors). Are any skirting boards cracked, uneven or showing other signs which may indicate rot or woodworm?

Access to under ground-floor areas; state of cellar or ground below – wet, dry, concreted, tiled or bare earth? Floor drains in any cellar – do they work? Damp/waterproofing between pillars and walls and joists/joist ends; signs of repair, rot, woodworm or fungus

Are staircases firm or shaky? If fixed to any wall or floor, is there rot or decay at the junction? Are windows easy to open or seized up by paint or other cause? Do they show any signs of rot, woodworm or decay?

Plumbing
Lead, plastic or copper pipework – if the last, is it old (half, three-quarter and one inch) or new (15, 22 and 38mm)? Three-quarter inch is not compatible with modern 22mm fittings but half (15mm) and inch (28mm) are; hot water cylinder insulated; water heating system and state and nature of any boilers; central heating system and state, nature and location of pipework, pumps, controls and radiators – pipes running through solid floors may be an extra corrosion risk; state of any baths, washbasins, sinks, loos and appliance connections; is the pipework earthed electrically (cables under taps) as it should be under modern regulations? Any signs of leaks at any pipework joins including radiators?

Electricity
White meter or ordinary; number and location of power points, light fittings, cooker and water heater controls; state and

apparent age of any exposed cabling; position of concealed cable runs – inspect any accessible; any obvious signs of DIY work

Telephone
Old (fixed) or modern (plug in) connection(s)

Heating and gas appliances
What is the state/modernity of appliances? Do all needing them have clear/safe flues? Are any flues lined or open to the fabric of the building? Is there any risk of toxic flue gases penetrating into the building? Does any timber or other combustible material project into the flues? Are there soot doors or other openings adequate to allow flues to be swept? If there are solar panels or heat pumps, do you have full technical details of them?

Further reading from Kogan Page

Going Freelance, Godfrey Golzen, 1989
How to Buy a Business, Second Edition, Peter Farrell, 1989
How to Buy and Renovate a Cottage, Stuart Turner, 1987
Running Your Own Pub, Elven Money, 1985
Running Your Own Small Hotel, Second Edition, Joy Lennick, 1989
Running Your Own Smallholding, Richard and Pauline Bambrey, 1989
Working For Yourself, Eleventh Edition, Godfrey Golzen, 1989

Index